Comments on other *Amazing Stories* from readers & reviewers

*"You might call them the non-fiction response to Harlequin
romances: easy to consume and potentially addictive."*
Robert Martin, *The Chronicle Herald*

*"Tightly written volumes filled with lots of wit and humour
about famous and infamous Canadians."*
Eric Shackleton, *The Globe and Mail*

*"This is popular history as it should be...
For this price, buy two and give one to a friend."*
Terry Cook, a reader from Ottawa, on **Rebel Women**

*"Stories are rich in description, and
bristle with a clever, stylish realness."*
Mark Weber, *Central Alberta Advisor*, on **Ghost Town Stories II**

*"The resulting book is one readers will want
to share with all the women in their lives."*
Lynn Martel, *Rocky Mountain Outlook*, on **Women Explorers**

"[The books are] *long on plot and character and short
on the sort of technical analysis that can be dreary
for all but the most committed academic."*
Robert Martin, *The Chronicle Herald*

*"A compelling read. Bertin ... has selected only the most intriguing
tales, which she narrates with a wealth of detail."*
Joyce Glasner, *New Brunswick Reader*, on **Strange Events**

*"The heightened sense of drama and intrigue, combined with a
good dose of human interest is what sets* Amazing Stories *apart."*
Pamela Klaffke, *Calgary Herald*

TITANIC

TITANIC

The Canadian Connection

HISTORY

by Lanny Boutin

PUBLISHED BY ALTITUDE PUBLISHING CANADA LTD.
1500 Railway Avenue, Canmore, Alberta T1W 1P6
www.altitudepublishing.com
www.amazingstories.ca
1-800-957-6888

Extreme care has been taken to ensure that all information presented in
this book is accurate and up to date. Neither the author nor the
publisher can be held responsible for any errors.

Publisher	Stephen Hutchings
Series Editor	Diana Marshall
Editors	Deborah Lawson and Lesley Cameron
Cover and Layout	Bryan Pezzi

We acknowledge the financial support of the Government
of Canada through the Book Publishing Industry Development
Program (BPIDP) for our publishing activities.

Altitude GreenTree Program
Altitude Publishing will plant twice as many trees as were used
in the manufacturing of this product.

National Library of Canada Cataloguing in Publication Data

Boutin, Lanny, 1958-
    Titanic : the Canadian connection / Lanny Boutin.

(Amazing stories)
ISBN 1-55439-126-1

    1. Titanic (Steamship). 2. Shipwrecks--North Atlantic Ocean.
I. Title. II. Series: Amazing stories (Canmore, Alta.)

G530.T6B69 2006   910.9163'4   C2006-903528-8

Printed and bound in Canada by Friesens
2 4 6 8 9 7 5 3 1

To
Bernie, Daniel, and Julia,
for all your patience and love.

Contents

Prologue
Forewarned

For a sheltered young woman from Winnipeg, Manitoba, it was the trip of a lifetime — traipsing around the world, visiting exotic locales such as Algeria, Monaco, Egypt, and Greece. And, being accustomed as she was to luxury, Alice Elizabeth Fortune was right at home among the throngs of wealthy travellers at the Shepheard Hotel, in Cairo, Egypt.

The Shepheard, with its lotus-topped pillars modelled after those of the legendary Karnak Temple, was one of the city's most celebrated landmarks. Located in the heart of British Cairo, it was a popular destination for the well-heeled. As for Cairo, in the early 1900s, it was a metropolitan oasis — the "Paris of the Nile." One of the world's largest cities, it was a vibrant mix of old and new. Modern tramways ran down ancient streets, with noisy, metallic wheels muffling the cries of merchants who still sold their wares in the Khan el Khalili souk, a fixture in the city since the 14th century.

Yes, Cairo was a magical, mystical place.

Alice and her friend William T. Sloper (a young stockbroker from New Britain, Connecticut, whom Alice had met on the trip over) set out in search of a shady spot where they could escape Cairo's muggy February heat and enjoy a cool drink. They found both at the hotel's vibrant Veranda Café.

But their shady spot overlooking the Nile was not as private as they might have hoped. Shortly after they sat down, a weathered little man begged Alice to come closer. Taking her hand, he slowly and meticulously examined her palm. Then, to her surprise, he declared that she was in grave danger, she would be in peril every time she travelled the sea. He saw her cast adrift in an open boat ...

Not one to believe superstitious tales, Alice paid the soothsayer and shrugged off his ominous warning. He vanished as quickly and as quietly as he had come.

It was indeed a fateful day, for little did Alice Fortune know that just two short months later, with the words of the fortuneteller all but forgotten, she would board a grand new ship: the Titanic.

Chapter 1
Brokers, Barons, and Bankers

L egends are built on dreams and J. Bruce Ismay had a big dream. On a quiet summer evening in 1907, Ismay, the managing director of the White Star Line, entered the London, England, home of Lord James Pirrie, a partner in the firm Harland and Wolff, one of Belfast's premier shipbuilders.

Ismay was bent on enlisting Pirrie's help. The Cunard Line, White Star's competition, was about to launch their new ship, the *Lusitania*, heating up the race for shipping supremacy in the Atlantic. That evening Pirrie and Ismay forged an alliance, and they agreed to build three gigantic ships. These ships would be the biggest and best in the world, packed with every luxury imaginable. They would be named the *Olympic*, the *Britannic*, and the *Titanic*.

* * *

At the start of the 20th century, Canada was experiencing a time of rapid growth fuelled by the dreams of men. It was quickly becoming a nation in its own right. Manitoba had just won provincial status, and Alberta and Saskatchewan were hot on its heels. A second transcontinental railway was in the works. A wireless message from Cornwall, England, to St. John's, Newfoundland, 3,380 kilometres away, signalled the start of a new communications age. And Anne of Green Gables, a fictional orphan girl with carrot-red hair, was about to introduce the world to the charm of a picturesque Canadian island.

It was a time of rapid growth, spurred on by the lure of free land for those not afraid of hard work. Immigration was exploding. In 1900 Canada's population was just more than five million people. Over the next 14 years almost three million immigrants landed on its shores.

A Fortune
It was also a time of winners and losers. Some settlers found the work overwhelming and returned home. But for most, the sweat, hard work, and ambition, and their willingness to take chances, paid off — frequently in a big way. Many went west with nothing and made it big. Mark Fortune was one of them.

From the start, Mark was determined to make something of his life. Born in 1847 on a farm near Carluke in

Wentworth County, Ontario, he packed his kit and headed to California while still in his teens. He landed in San Francisco, drawn by the lure of the gold rush. But unlike the Klondike, California was not teeming with gold. Of the hundreds of men and women who travelled south, only a select few made it big. Mark returned to Canada in 1871 — certainly no worse for wear, but no richer, either.

Not one to give up, Mark headed to Manitoba, Canada's newest province. He eventually found himself in Upper Fort Garry, a settlement of 219 people. The Northwest Rebellion had just been quashed, and the government was systematically stripping the Métis people of their land. The brazen and self-confident young man swooped in, buying up large tracts of cheap land along the Assiniboine River. He believed this area would one day be the hub of the province. Some laughed at his vision, but his belief was unwavering.

In 1873 the Red River colony of Upper Fort Garry merged with the fur trading station, creating the city of Winnipeg. A year later the railroad rounded the south end of Lake Manitoba and chugged down to Winnipeg. The boom was on, and Mark's speculations finally paid off. Portage Avenue, Winnipeg's main thoroughfare, ran right through his land.

Mark dabbled in politics, serving as a city councillor in the ward of Winnipeg West from 1879 to 1881, and in Ward Two in 1883. Winnipeg was growing rapidly, and by 1884 numerous new businesses were searching for office space. Mark constructed the three-storey Fortune Block at the corner of St. Mary Avenue and Main Street. Two years later Winnipeg's population hit 30,000.

In 1910 Mark commissioned a 36-room Tudor-style stone and stucco mansion for his wife, Mary (née McDougald), at 393 Wellington Crescent in one of Winnipeg's most prestigious neighbourhoods. A year later, when his youngest son, Charles, graduated from Bishop's College School in Lennoxville with honours in both academics and athletics, Mark treated his family to a grand tour of Europe. The two oldest children, Robert and Clara, declined the invitation, but the other Fortune children — daughters Ethel Flora, Alice Elizabeth, and Mabel Helen, and son Charles Alexander — eagerly accompanied their parents on this once-in-a-lifetime adventure.

On January 8, 1912, the Fortune family left Winnipeg for New York by train. They travelled with three of Mark's friends and business acquaintances, known as "the Winnipeg Musketeers." The trio consisted of Thomas Beattie (a 36-year-old land developer), Beattie's best friend and travel companion, 46-year-old Thomas McCaffry (originally a Winnipeg boy, McCaffry had become manager and western superintendent of the Vancouver Union Bank), and Hugo Ross, aged 36 (son of Arthur Wellington Ross, the late Liberal-Conservative member of parliament for the Manitoba constituency of Lisgar). On January 20, they boarded the Cunard liner *Fanconia,* heading for Trieste, in what was then the Austro-Hungarian Empire.

A Broker

Winnipeg wasn't the only Canadian city experiencing a building boom at the turn of the century. Montreal, Quebec, was growing rapidly in both size and influence. In 1901 it was the country's largest city, with a population in excess of 267,000. The residents of this bustling island situated on the St. Lawrence River controlled close to 70 percent of Canada's wealth. It was tailor-made for someone like Hudson Allison.

It was said that Hudson Joshua Creighton Allison was born with his strong Protestant work ethic. Born on December 9, 1881, Hudson was raised in a modest brick farmhouse on Finch Road, just east of Chesterville, Ontario, about 50 kilometres southeast of Ottawa.

Hud, as he was affectionately known, was very good with figures. While still in his teens he landed a clerk's job at Chester Casselman's general store in Chesterville. By the age of 19, the slender and often sombre young man was off to Montreal to head the junior division of a brokerage firm owned by his uncle, George Frank Johnston. Hud was quickly accepted into Montreal's "Methodist Mafia," a prestigious group of financial up-and-comers.

Hud also spent several years in Winnipeg setting up an insurance office. During this time he met both Mark Fortune and Thomas Beattie. It was during one of Hud's frequent train trips back to Montreal that he spotted Bess Waldo Daniels. Bess, who was born on November 14, 1886, was the youngest daughter of Arville Daniels, an Irish-American factory clerk from Milwaukee, Wisconsin. Bess was a quiet, graceful, reserved young woman. She and Hud instantly hit it off.

Hud was quite a catch. In 1912 he was said to be worth several million dollars. In spite of that, though, Bess's parents didn't seem impressed with their future son-in-law. Nonetheless, against her parents' wishes, Bess and Hud were married in Milwaukee on Hud's birthday in 1907. On their return to Montreal, Hud was given a full partnership in his uncle's brokerage firm. Their daughter, Helen Loraine (known as Loraine), was born on June 5, 1909, followed by a son, Hudson Trevor (known as Trevor), two years later on May 7, 1911.

Devout Methodists, Bess and Hud embraced the temperance movement, staunchly supporting its rejection of alcohol. They taught Sunday school and Bible classes; Hud even occasionally served as a lay preacher.

In 1911 the Allisons began construction of their new home at 1085 Belmont Avenue in Westmount, Quebec. They also owned a residence in London, England, and a summer home on Lake St. Louis. Together with his brothers Percy and George, Hud purchased their family's original homestead and an extra 100 acres of land from a nearby farmer. He immediately constructed a huge farmhouse, much larger than the one the boys had grown up in. He built numerous barns and outbuildings, which he stocked with imported Hackney ponies, Clydesdale horses, and Friesian cattle. It was reported that Hud had paid the previously unheard-of sum of $1,500 for May Echo, a Holstein-Friesian cow.

In December 1911 the Allisons sailed to England. Hud was to attend the directors' meeting of the British Lumber Corporation, while Bess planned to spend her time browsing antique shops and fabric manufacturers in search of treasures to decorate their homes.

When the meeting wrapped up the family travelled to Epworth, Lincolnshire, to have Trevor baptized in the church where famed Methodist founder John Wesley had preached. They then headed to the Scottish Highlands where Hud purchased two dozen prize stallions and mares of Clydesdale and Hackney bloodlines.

While abroad, the Allisons also hired several new staff members. Nineteen-year-old George Swane was hired as a chauffeur, 18-year-old Mildred Brown was hired as a cook, and 22-year-old Alice Cleaver replaced little Trevor's nursemaid, who had left abruptly.

A Baron

Another prominent Montreal businessman, Charles Melville Hays, was also in England, attending the board of directors' meetings of the Grand Trunk Central Railroad Company. An American by birth, the soft-spoken, 55-year-old Hays was president of the Canadian arm of the company.

Charles had started his career with the Atlantic and Pacific Railway when he was just 17, and by the age of 22 he was secretary to the manager of the Missouri Pacific Railway. Three years later he married Clara Gregg with whom he had four daughters.

An extremely intelligent man and a hard worker, Charles was appointed general manager of the entire Wabash Railway network in 1889. Six year later J. P. Morgan, the American banker who eventually acquired the White Star Line, recommended Charles for the general manager position of Canada's Grand Trunk Pacific Railway. Charles accepted and moved his family to Montreal. By 1910 he was a member of the Grand Trunk's board of directors and president of the company.

As president, Charles received the healthy salary of $25,000 per year — this at a time when the average supervisor in Canada only earned around $1,000 per year. But Charles worked very long hours to stay on top and realize his dreams.

One of those dreams was to break the monopoly held by the Canadian Pacific Railway by building a second rail line from Moncton, New Brunswick, to Prince Rupert, British Columbia — a span of almost 6,000 kilometres. The Liberal government of Prime Minister Sir Wilfrid Laurier was sceptical, but Charles would not be dissuaded.

Originally the government had been adamant that the Grand Trunk must bear the full financial burden for the new rail line. But with passion and perseverance, Charles slowly ground them down. Not only did he convince the politicians that Canada desperately needed a second transcontinental railroad, he even convinced them to pay for it! Eventually the government agreed to build the complete line from Winnipeg to Moncton and lease it back to the Grand Trunk. Charles also persuaded them to underwrite much of the cost of the rest of the line by convincing them to invest another $30 million in the scheme. By November of 1902 construction had begun on Canada's second cross-country rail line.

In England, the Grand Trunk's board of directors remained sceptical. Even with government money, by the end of 1911 the Canadian arm of the railway was $100 million in debt. None of this concerned Charles, however; he believed the company could simply spend its way out of bankruptcy by upgrading the rolling stock, doubling the tracking, and constructing a chain of luxury hotels across Canada — starting with the elegant, copper-topped, French Renaissance–style Château Laurier on Rideau Street in Ottawa. It was in the hope of persuading the parent company to approve his lavish spending scheme that he and his family had ventured forth to England.

A Banker

Not everyone living in Montreal at the turn of the century felt included in the city's booming business and social scene. Montreal was a city deeply divided along racial, cultural, and religious lines. And some — particularly English-speaking Protestant Montrealers such as Jim Baxter — felt emotionally and economically isolated.

"Diamond Jim," as he was known to both friends and enemies, was a banker and diamond broker. Born into a poor Irish Protestant family, Jim was determined to raise his social status. In August of 1882, he married Hélène de Lanaudière-Chaput, from Joliette, Quebec. Hélène's family, although no longer rich, claimed to be direct descendants of the French Canadian heroine Madeline de Verchères. Legend has it that Madeline, in 1692, had tricked a large Iroquois war party into believing that the unarmed stockade was actually heavily guarded. The Iroquois retreated, and the stockade was saved. In gratitude, her family was given title of the entire county of Lanaudière, northeast of Montreal.

Driven by his young wife's desire for the finer things in life, Jim built her a mansion in one of Montreal's most prestigious areas, an enclave nicknamed "the Square Mile" by Montreal's Scottish Presbyterians. Jim's gigantic three-storey greystone house at 1201 Sherbrooke Street West, which looked more like an apartment block than a single home, put the Baxters right in the middle of Montreal's wealthy set. But in spite of their growing affluence, the Baxters and their three children, Anthony William, Mary ("Zette") Hélène, and Quigg Edmond, still did not fit in.

In 1892 Jim built the Baxter Block, Canada's first shopping mall. It consisted of 28 stores under one roof. He also opened his own private bank. In 1898, *Men in Canada* described him as Canada's largest private banker and praised

him for devoting much of his wealth to improving the outly-
ing districts of Montreal.

However not everything was as it should have been. The
first indication of wrongdoing came when Jim was accused
of violating United States currency exchange rules. Then, in
1900, he was charged with embezzling $40,000 from his own
bank, the Banque Ville Marie, which had closed one year
earlier. In a spectacular trial Jim was convicted of embezzle-
ment and consequently spent five years in jail. Released in
1905, just three weeks short of his 66th birthday, he opened a
diamond and financial brokerage house in the Baxter Block.
But the years of incarceration had taken their toll, and Jim
died shortly after his release.

The Montreal newspapers had a heyday, reporting that
Jim had died penniless, which was far from the truth. His
numerous investments in France, Switzerland, and Belgium
had left Hélène and the children well provided for.

Hélène sold the mansion and moved into a comfortable
brownstone at 33 St. Famille Street, near McGill University.
Over the next few years she took numerous trips to Europe to
monitor her investments. She left Montreal every autumn, at
the start of the social season, preferring to spend her winters
in France. In 1911 she sold the Baxter Block and travelled to
Europe in search of medical treatment for a heart condition.
Her son Quigg and her now-married daughter, Zette Douglas,
accompanied her.

Chapter 2
First Class
All the Way

The Fortune family and their entourage had a grand time in Europe. After landing in Trieste, they travelled through Greece, crossing the Mediterranean to Jerusalem. They fed pigeons in St. Mark's Square in Venice, visited the Karnak Temple at Luxor, and saw the great Sphinx of Giza. The last leg of their trip brought them to London and the Carlton Hotel where, on Easter Sunday, April 7, 1912, they threw themselves a lavish bon voyage party. The girls, Ethel, Alice, and Mabel, appeared in their elegant new Worth gowns from Paris — all in primrose pink, the season's most stylish colour. Each girl sported a pearl choker, the latest European jewellery craze.

Even with all the merriment it was difficult to hide the fact that they were exhausted and looking forward to going home. Ethel was eager to return to her fiancé, Toronto banker Crawford Gordon, since, at the urging of the Fortune parents, the couple had postponed their wedding so Ethel could travel abroad with her family and chaperone her younger siblings. Mabel was anxious to be reunited with her first love, Harrison Driscoll, a jazz musician from Minnesota whom Mabel's parents had desperately hoped their daughter would forget while in Europe. Hugo Ross and Thomas Beattie were also anxious to get back to Winnipeg. Both were ill and feeling quite exhausted.

Before leaving Paris, Mark Fortune had decided to change the group's return travel plans. Instead of returning on the Cunard liner *Mauretania*, Mark booked cabins on the maiden voyage of the newest ship of the White Star Line — a ship portrayed in advertisements as being the largest and most luxurious ship on the sea: RMS *Titanic*. Beattie wrote his mother back home in Canada, telling her how excited he was to be travelling on this new, "unsinkable" ship.

William Sloper ran into Alice Fortune again in London. He secretly decided to cancel his return ticket on the *Mauretania* and instead travel back with the Fortunes on the *Titanic*. When Alice heard of his change in plans she teasingly reminded him of the dangers of travelling with her. Had he forgotten the words of the fortuneteller? Was he really willing to be stranded with her ... thrown adrift on the sea? Amused, Sloper light-heartedly mocked her; didn't she know that the fortuneteller said that to all the rich Canadian girls?

Subsequently, in the early morning hours of April 10, 1912, Sloper joined the Fortune family and their weary band of fellow travellers at London's Waterloo Station. There they boarded the boat train to the Southampton docks, almost 120 kilometres away. It was a crisp, sunny day — perfect for a train ride through the lovely English countryside. The travellers were treated to spectacular views of lush green fields, with animals grazing contently among long rows of budding green hedges.

Meanwhile, at Southampton's Dock 44, the *Titanic* was being prepared. The gigantic ship towered almost 11 storeys above a long procession of firemen, trimmers, greasers, stewards, and others making their way along the dock below. Its shiny black hull stretched for four city blocks; it was almost as wide as a hockey rink and weighed in at 46,300 tons.

Longshoremen loaded the ship with hundreds of delicacies, including almost 11,000 pounds of fresh fish, 1,750 pounds of ice cream, and 6,000 pounds of butter. There were also 1,500 bottles of wine, 36,000 oranges, and 2 tons of tomatoes. The ship carried 100 pairs of grape scissors and 400 asparagus tongs to go with her 12,000 dinner plates. Place settings for the first-class dining room were handmade from the finest white bone china; their scalloped edges, gilded in 24-karat gold, were surrounded a delicate turquoise-and-brown Wisteria pattern, with the White Star Line's emblem and red pennant embossed on their centre.

By 7 a.m., when Captain Edward John Smith, decked

out in his bowler hat and overcoat, stepped from his taxi, most of the *Titanic's* supplies had already been safely stowed. Captain Smith had started his seafaring career on a clipper ship, the *Senatro Webe*, at age 13. He joined the White Star Line in 1880, at the age of 30, as a fourth officer. Over the years he had commanded 17 White Star ships, including the *Majestic*, the *Baltic*, and *Titanic's* sister ship, the *Olympic*.

Soft-spoken and self-assured, Smith was considered by some to be the "millionaires' captain." He piloted only the best and newest ships in the White Star Line. It was rumoured that of all the jobs required of a captain, entertaining the passengers — especially the rich ones — was his favourite. He was an honorary commander of the Royal Naval Reserve and, as such, flew the Blue Ensign on all the merchant vessels he commanded. At age 62 he was ready for retirement. In fact, Smith had planned that the maiden voyage of the *Titanic* would be his last.

One of the first passengers to arrive that morning was Joseph Ismay. He and his family pulled up to the dock in his Daimler Landaulette touring car. They were just back from a motoring holiday through Wales and had spent the night at the Southampton South Western Hotel, which overlooked Dock 44 and the *Titanic*.

As the morning progressed the *Titanic's* siren rang out periodically, adding to the overall chaos and reminding everyone for miles around that today was her sailing day. Soon, local passengers began arriving on foot, and by car and bus. People swarmed the dock, luggage in tow. Families struggled to stay together as they made their way through the growing crowd. The boat trains, which carried first-, second-, and third-class passengers from London, began arriving around 9:30 a.m. The Fortunes, like other boat-train passengers, were transferred directly to their gangway and onto the ship.

From there they followed a steward to their cabins. The Fortunes had booked a block of three outside starboard cabins — numbers 23, 25, and 27 along C deck. Beattie and McCaffry were rooming together in a forward port-side cabin, C6. Hugo Ross was by this time so ill with dysentery that they had to carry him aboard on a stretcher. He opted for an inside port-side cabin, number 10 on A deck, close to the Grand Staircase entrance.

On B deck, directly above the Fortune's cabins, Charles Hays and his family were also settling in. Charles was eagerly anticipating one of his pet projects — the April 26 grand opening of his Château Laurier Hotel. He had with him a notebook containing the description of six other luxury hotels he planned to build. These included the Lord Selkirk (now the Fort Garry) Hotel in Winnipeg, the Château Qu'Appelle in Regina, the Château Miette and Mount Robson in the Canadian Rockies, the Grand Trunk Pacific Railway Hotel in Prince Rupert, and the Macdonald Hotel in Edmonton.

Clara Fortune was also anxious to get home. While in England they'd received word that one of their daughters was experiencing complications with her pregnancy. Doctors said that Louise, whose baby was due some time in April, might require a caesarean section. Clara desperately wanted to be there with her.

The Hays family had boarded the *Titanic* as guests of Joseph Ismay. In his capacity as director of the London North Railway and managing director of the White Star Line, Ismay had spoken to Charles Hays on many occasions about how their respective companies could work together.

Charles paid 93 pounds Sterling, 10 shillings (about $16,000 in year-2000 dollars) to cover only the incidental expenses for their four cabins. Charles and Clara's cabin, B69, was midship on the *Titanic's* starboard side; their daughter, Orian, and her husband, Thornton Davidson, were next door in cabin B71. Clara's maid, Miss Perreault, was near the front of the ship in cabin B24, and Charles's friend and personal secretary, Vivian Payne, had cabin B73, an inside cabin next to the Davidsons. For 23-year-old Payne it was the trip of a lifetime — his first trip abroad.

On the other side of the ship, in one of the nicer parlour suites, which, incidentally, was one of the few cabins to be photographed, the Baxter family was unpacking. Hélène Baxter had laid out 247 pounds Sterling, 10 shillings, 5 pence for her family's tickets (the equivalent of more than $40,000 in year-2000 dollars).

The Baxter suite consisted of two bedrooms, each with its own sitting area. The *Titanic's* first-class bedrooms were bright and spacious, each decorated in a different and distinct style, ranging from Italian Renaissance to Queen Anne, their silken bedspreads and extra-wide beds adding to their comfort. Quigg's room held a raised-panel wooden bed, stained dark to match the elaborate wall and door trim. Hélène and Zette's room sported a wrought-iron Waterford-type bed and brocade pillows that accented the delicately carved and stencilled two-tone trim. But theirs was not the best suite on the ship. That was reserved for J. Bruce Ismay. His suite, located right next to that of the Baxters, was one of the two "millionaire suites," each with its own, private, 50-foot (15-metre) promenade deck.

The suites and cabins on the *Titanic* also contained many modern electrical conveniences such as gimbal lamps designed to stay level on the roughest of seas, heaters, table fans, steward call bells, and electrical blowers that brought fresh air in from outside. Some cabins even had their own telephones.

When Hud and Bess Allison heard that many of their friends were travelling back to North America aboard a wonderful new luxury ship, they also altered their travel plans. Hud paid £151, 16 shillings for (it is believed) three cabins on C deck port side. Hud, Bess, and Loraine probably occupied the outside cabins, C26 and C24, while Trevor, his nursemaid, Miss Cleaver, and Bess's maid, Miss Daniels, probably stayed in the inside cabin, C22. The rest of the Allison staff travelled below in second class.

Shortly before noon the *Titanic's* siren sounded, this time to advise staff and passengers of her impending departure. Visitors, shore staff, and harbour officials quickly concluded their business and disembarked.

At noon, the ship's whistle blew three times and her gangways were slowly withdrawn. With thousands of well-wishers cheering, her seven-piece band playing, and the help of six tugs, the ship slowly inched her way into the shipping lane. Passengers threw flowers from the ship to the dock. A profusion of colourful scarves and handkerchiefs waved back.

On deck, taking in all the excitement, was Major Arthur Godfrey Peuchen. A 52-year-old major in the Queen's Own Rifles, Peuchen was travelling alone. His wife, Margaret, and two teenaged children waited for him in Canada. Originally from Montreal, Peuchen had moved to Toronto to join the Queen's Own Rifles. He moved up the ranks quickly, making lieutenant in 1888, captain in 1894, and major by 1904. In 1911 he had the honour of being the marshalling officer at the coronation of King George V.

Peuchen was the president of the Standard Chemical Company, one of the first companies in the world to manufacture acetone, used in explosives, out of wood. He also owned large tracts of forest reserve land near Hinton, Alberta.

The family had a house at 599 Jarvis Street in Toronto, but Peuchen spent most of his time at their cottage on Lake Simcoe, about 80 kilometres north. This lakeside estate, which he called the Woodlands, boasted tennis courts, a golf course, and a marina where he docked his 38-ton, almost 20-metre yacht, the *Vreda*. The vice-commodore of the Royal Canadian Yacht Club, Peuchen was no stranger to transatlantic travel — this trip was his 40th crossing. Tall, erect, and athletic, Peuchen was not one to put on airs. He had reserved a basic corner cabin, C104, with neither a porthole nor a private bath.

Shortly after the *Titanic* pulled away from the pier, Peuchen noticed that its wash, or suction, was causing havoc among the other boats tethered along the route. Then he heard a chorus of loud snapping sounds, a sound some on the ship mistook for gunshots. But it was really the sound of mooring lines snapping. The *Titanic*'s turbulent wake caused all six of the mooring lines securing the liner *New York* to break. Large coils of rope hurled themselves high into the air then ricocheted back down onto the crowded dock. No longer secure, and with her crew no longer in control, the *New York* first swung out toward the *Titanic*'s stern, and then drifted toward the gigantic ship's bow.

Officers on the *Titanic* ordered a "full astern." The waves created by her port propeller drove the *New York* away. The two boats missed by only metres.

The tug *Vulcan*, which had just cast off from the *Titanic*'s bow, raced back to help push the *New York* out of the *Titanic*'s way. It took almost three-quarters of an hour to straighten out the mess. But eventually the *Titanic* resumed its 40-kilometre trip down the English Channel on its way to Cherbourg, France. The news of the near-collision spread quickly through the ship. Some, no doubt, considered it an ominous start to their trip.

Because of the delay, it was suppertime before the *Titanic* reached Cherbourg. Her size forced her to drop anchor far out in the harbour and wait for the White Star tender, the *Nomadic*, to ferry passengers and cargo out. By 8:10 p.m. she had raised her anchor and headed back down the channel toward her last stop at Queenstown, Cobh, in Cork Harbour, Ireland. On Thursday morning she again dropped anchor, this time by Roches Point, where more passengers boarded and cargo, including hundreds of bolts of Irish lace and linen, were stowed. Finally, the *Titanic* lifted anchor. With the steeple of St. Coleman's Cathedral disappearing behind her, she rounded the grey cliffs of Ireland's misty shoreline and headed for the open sea.

Chapter 3
On the Open Sea

Once out on the open sea, the ship settled into a predictable pattern, and the passengers settled into a comfortable routine. There was so much to do on the ship. Men started their days with a hot shave in the first-class barbershop. Peuchen and Hays spent much of their spare time working out in the gymnasium on the boat deck. There was also a heated saltwater swimming pool, the first ever aboard a ship, and squash courts. For a dollar, you could soak in the Turkish bath or relax in its richly decorated cooling room. The gym instructor was an Englishman named T. W. McCawley, whom Charles praised for his tireless enthusiasm. McCawley was always available to educate anyone interested in the proper use of the gym equipment. He spoke passionately about the modern electric horses, electric camels, and the weightlifting and rowing devices.

In the afternoons, the men often retired to the first-class smoking room, and the ladies went off to the reading and writing room next door. Little ones, like Loraine Allison and her six-year-old friend Robert Douglas Spedden, treated the palm room, with its ivy-covered walls and white wicker furniture, as their own private playground. Many of the young adults on board, like Quigg Baxter, hung out at the Café Parisienne.

A small, bright, airy café on B deck, the Parisienne was modelled after real Parisian sidewalk cafés, with casual French décor and authentic French waiters. It was a wonderful place to spend an afternoon enjoying pastis and strong coffee. Its large picture windows offered a spectacular view of the ocean and, when the weather allowed, could be rolled down, permitting passengers to dine al fresco, another first for the *Titanic*.

A scar-faced young man of 24, Quigg had a lopsided grin that gave him a boyish charm. He'd dropped out of his first year of applied science at McGill University to accompany his mother to Europe and check on his many hockey interests. A remarkable athlete, Quigg joined the Montreal Amateur Athletic Association at the age of 17 and quickly proved to be a rising star in both football and hockey. He played for the Montreal Shamrocks hockey team until 1907, when he was blinded in one eye by an opponent's stick. In 1909, consumed by his love of hockey but no longer able to play, he tried his hand at coaching. That same year he travelled to Europe to help organize the first international hockey tournaments in France and Switzerland.

While abroad, Quigg encountered a fascinating but mysterious young woman, Mrs. B. de Villiers. The robust young woman with dark, wavy hair and deep brooding eyes, whose real name was Berthe Antonine Mayné, rapidly charmed her way into Quigg's life. She boarded the *Titanic* on a ticket she said had been purchased by Quigg. Her intent, it seemed, was to travel to Montreal and become Quigg's bride.

Quigg, however, had conveniently neglected to mention any of this to his mother or sister. He likely believed (probably correctly) that his mother's strong sense of social rank would keep her from giving them her blessing. Berthe was not a typical, cultured European young lady. Indeed, she possessed many qualities that Hélène Baxter was probably not looking for in a daughter-in-law. She was a cabaret singer who, in the hope of reinventing herself, had adopted the name de Villiers, a name with aristocratic Belgian lineage. Even more scandalous, Berthe was known in Brussels' "circles of pleasure."

It was therefore not surprising that this headstrong young man with a notorious lust for life had the gall to smuggle his fiancée on board without telling his mother. As it turned out, hiding Berthe was easier than he had hoped, since Hélène was confined to her cabin, fighting off a bad bout of seasickness.

The *Titanic*'s maiden voyage was going remarkably well. The weather was fine, the wind and sea calm. The ship was making especially good time, running steadily at a speed of more than 22 knots. There was even talk of getting to New York a day early.

The only problem that had arisen was with the wireless telecommunication equipment. One of the first ships to be fitted with a full Marconi wireless system, the *Titanic* had the ability to be in constant contact with other ships or land stations. But early on Saturday evening the equipment failed. Messages were piling up from passengers wishing to contact friends and family in North America. The two wireless operators, employees of the Marconi Company, worked frantically, doing everything they could to get the equipment up and running again. They were especially anxious to get it working in time to take advantage of Sunday's close proximity to the coast of Newfoundland and the Cape Race transmitter. This transmitter offered them a direct way to relay passengers' messages to New York. The wireless operators put in a long, sleepless night. Finally, by approximately five o'clock on Sunday morning, everything was working again.

Sunday breakfast was served, bright and early as usual, in the dining room. But many first-class passengers decided not to "dress" for breakfast. Instead they opted for a leisurely morning meal in the saloon. Some finished up with a long walk on deck, admiring the vastness of the ocean; others remained in the saloon, discussing politics and marvelling at their wonderful crossing.

At 10:30 a.m., Captain Smith led a devotional service for the first-class passengers. He started with passages from a prayer book printed especially for the *Titanic*. He then encouraged everyone to join him in a hymn sing, ending with a few stanzas of "O God, Our Help in Ages Past," an old favourite by hymn writer Isaac Watts. With the benediction complete, the passengers retired to their cabins to dress for lunch. First-class passengers typically came on board with as many as 20 bags and, according to the custom of the day, changed their clothing for each meal or activity.

After lunch Captain Smith headed to the bridge to supervise the ship's weekly lifeboat drill. A White Star tradition, every Sunday morning while at sea one lifeboat on each side of the ship was uncovered, swung out over the side of the ship, and boarded by a crew member. But Smith noticed the wind was picking up and, being confident that everything was fine, decided the lifeboat drill was unnecessary. So he cancelled it.

Most of the passengers were now getting excited about reaching New York. George Graham, a buyer for the T. Eaton Company in Toronto, sent a cable to his wife saying he'd be home on Wednesday morning. Mark Fortune telegraphed the Belmont Hotel in New York, asking them to reserve two double rooms with baths, as well as a single room.

Around 5 p.m., passengers started heading to their

cabins to freshen up and dress for dinner. It had been a brisk but pleasant 6 degrees Celsius during the day, but as evening approached the temperature dropped rapidly. By suppertime it was close to zero.

Captain Smith went to the bridge to go over the evening's orders. The ship was just about to reach "the corner," a spot near the Great Banks of Newfoundland at latitude 42°N, longitude 47°W, where ships normally adjusted their southwestern route and travelled almost due west toward the Nantucket Lightship. But Smith decided, likely on account of the numerous ice warnings they'd received over the previous few days, to maintain the *Titanic*'s original southwestern route for another 45 minutes. This, he hoped, would keep the *Titanic* south of the ice.

Satisfied that his orders were noted and everything was under control, Smith headed to his cabin to dress for a special reception in his honour, hosted by Philadelphia streetcar magnate George D. Widener. Around 7 p.m., Peuchen, who was heading to his cabin to change, passed the formally dressed Smith in the corridor. Shortly after, Peuchen joined Hud, Bess, and his friend Harry Molson for supper in the first-class dining saloon.

Peuchen had been previously acquainted with many of the other Canadians on board. He already knew Hugo Ross who, as a student at the University of Toronto, had been part of Peuchen's yacht crew. Through travels and business dealings over the years he had become acquainted with Mark

Fortune, Thomas Beattie, and Thomas McCaffry, as well as with Charles Hays and Thornton Davidson. Peuchen knew the Allison family, and he was best friends with Molson.

Molson, 55, was probably the richest Canadian on board. The great-grandson of John Molson (founder of the Molson beer, banking, and steamship empires), the middle-aged Harry was a bachelor who, although unpretentious in manner, invariably dressed in a smart, dapper fashion, and always kept his ample beard neatly trimmed. He was extremely fond of expensive cigars, golden pocket watches, and a lucky horseshoe-shaped diamond stickpin given to him by a lady friend.

Molson had his fingers in many pies. He sat on the board of directors of the Molson Bank, the Canadian Transfer Company, and the Standard Chemical Company. He'd been elected to city council in 1902, and served as Dorval's mayor from 1903 to 1905. He was Worshipful Master of Quebec's oldest Masonic Lodge, St. Paul's Lodge #374, a commodore of the Royal St. Lawrence Yacht Club, and a founding member of the Forest and Stream Club. Harry also sat as governor of the Montreal General Hospital and president of the Canadian Society for the Prevention of Cruelty to Animals (CSPCA), a cause that was especially close to his heart.

"Merry Larkwand" Molson, as his friends often called him, was an avid yachtsman. His 40-ton, almost 23-metre yacht, the *Alcyone*, was stored at his summer home in Dorval. He was also a veteran of accidents at sea. In 1899 he survived the sinking of the *Scotsman* in the Gulf of St. Lawrence. In 1904, wearing only his shirt and trousers, he swam to shore after the *Canada* collided with a coal ship in the St. Lawrence River near Sorel. The *Titanic* would give him his third encounter with the sea.

At a little more than 30 metres in length, the *Titanic's* first-class dining room was the largest room on any ship at the time. Located midship at the bottom of the Grand Staircase, the 500-plus seat dining room boasted numerous Jacobean-styled alcoves with leaded glass windows around its perimeter, which allowed light to stream in from the outside passageway. The room was so elegant that Bess Allison brought Loraine in for a brief tour just before supper that Sunday night.

Supper on board the ship was always a leisurely affair. Peuchen later recalled appreciatively that Sunday's supper had been exceptionally good. The appetizer course had consisted of oysters and other assorted hors d'oeuvres. Main course choices in the first-class dining room had comprised 17 different items including such dishes as salmon and cucumber in mousseline sauce, lamb in mint sauce, filet mignons lili, and pâté de foie gras. For dessert, passengers could choose from Waldorf pudding, peaches in chartreuse jelly, chocolate and vanilla éclairs, and French ice cream.

As friends talked, the tables were cleared and replenished with each new course. Wine glasses were emptied and refilled, the haunting sound of the orchestra filling the air. The

Fortune family enjoyed a relaxing family dinner. The Baxters, oblivious to the social gaff Zette was making by wearing a diamond and silver tiara to supper (tiaras as adornments had fallen out of favour in first-class circles of the time), sat across the room, their language separating them from other passengers.

Just before 9 p.m. Captain Smith excused himself and headed back to the bridge, to check in one more time. Smith and First Officer Charles Herbert Lightoller stood on deck conversing quietly. Confident everything was under control, Smith retired to his cabin.

About the same time, Peuchen and Molson headed out to a small sitting room just outside the main dining room, each sinking into a white wicker armchair to enjoy a leisurely cup of coffee. The Allisons declined their friends' invitation to join them for coffee and instead went to their cabin to check on the children and prepare for bed. Charles and Clara joined some other passengers strolling along the boat deck, enjoying the beautiful crimson sunset. Clara was amazed at how clear the night was and how calm the ocean seemed. Stars twinkled brilliantly against the dark night sky, the black water seeming to reach out and touch them.

Even at night there was plenty to do on the ship. Passengers congregated in the palm room to enjoy a cup of coffee and listen to the *Titanic*'s orchestra, which was known for its wide repertoire. Its playbill included 120 overtures and many operatic selections, as well as waltzes, suites, and fantasies. The music that night was especially beautiful, people later recalled, with the orchestra performance approaching the quality of an actual concert.

Their coffee finished, Peuchen and Molson moved to the first-class smoking room. There they found Beattie and McCaffry. The four men chatted, smoked cigars, and shared a glass or two of cognac until about 11:20 p.m., when Peuchen bade them goodnight and retired to his cabin.

After seeing Clara safely to their room, Charles joined Colonel Archibald Butt, the military aide to President William Howard Taft and former President Theodore Roosevelt in the smoking room. The room's mahogany-panelled walls with leaded glass inserts, etched glass mirrors, and leather barrel armchairs clustered around small marble-topped tables, made a peaceful and inviting place for serious conversation. As the night wore on the discussions probably touched on world politics as well as Charles's favourite topic: trains. They even discussed the fragile nature of sea travel. Charles voiced his concern over the fierce competition between the White Star, Cunard, and Hamburg shipping lines, which he felt were devoting excessive time and effort toward outdoing one another. Charles expressed his sincere belief that if the obsession with luxury and speed records didn't stop, the time would come — and soon — when they would be faced with a dreadful disaster.

Chapter 4
Danger Ahead

s the night wore on, stewards tidied and closed the ship's numerous salons and cafés. By 11:30 p.m. only the first- and second-class smoking rooms were still occupied.

Up on the boat deck the crew was readying the ship for the night. With the temperature dropping so dramatically they had to take precautions to keep the fresh water supply from freezing. The Marconi operators worked at top speed to catch up on the backlog of passengers' messages.

Since leaving port the *Titanic* had received close to 20 warnings about ice in the shipping lanes. At 1:45 on Sunday afternoon they received a cable from the *Amerika*, reporting a 120-kilometre band of ice directly in the *Titanic*'s path. The *Amerika*'s message was given to Ismay. He put it in his pocket and forgot about it. At 7:30 p.m. the wireless opera-tor on the *Californian* broadcast a message to all ships in the area, reporting large icebergs in the shipping lane ahead. This message was delivered to the bridge, but it is believed that Captain Smith, who was still at supper, never received it. The last warning was received shortly after 9:30 p.m. from the steamer *Mesaba,* whose wireless operator reported a large ice field with a lot of icebergs, located between latitudes 42° N and 41°23' N, and between longitudes 49° W and 50°3' W — again, right in the ship's path. But the *Titanic's* wireless operator, trying frantically to catch up on his work, set the message aside. It never made it to the bridge.

About 11:05 p.m. Cyril Evans, wireless operator on the *Californian,* attempted once again to advise the *Titanic* of the numerous ice floes now surrounding the ship. Evans was instantly rebuffed by *Titanic* wireless operator John Phillips, who cut him off, saying, "Shut up, shut up, I'm busy." Evans, stunned by his colleague's rudeness, decided to call it a night. He turned off his wireless equipment, a normal practice at the time, and went to bed.

Even without the most recent warnings, bridge officers were still expecting to encounter ice that night. Earlier, Sixth Officer James Paul Moody had reminded the lookouts to keep a sharp eye out for ice. But the lookouts, situated high up in the crow's nest more than 36 metres forward from the bridge, were working without the aid of binoculars. Back in port, when David Blair was bumped at the last minute to accommodate Officer Henry Wilde, Blair had neglected to tell anyone that the binoculars were stashed in his locker.

Icebergs are a common sight in the North Atlantic shipping lanes, but in the spring of 1912 they were particularly abundant. The exceptionally mild winter in the Arctic and the northern gales were pushing large quantities of heavy pack ice down the Labrador Current. Many seasoned sailors said they had never before seen ice so far south.

As the sun set that night, the wind dropped and the sea became perfectly calm. There was only a sliver of moon, making it virtually impossible to spot icebergs, especially black ones, from any distance. Black icebergs (or blue icebergs as they are sometimes called) are ones that have recently flipped over in the water, exposing their saturated bottoms. For several days, until all the sea water drains, they look dark. They are virtually impossible to spot at night.

Around 11:40 p.m. lookout Frederick Fleet noticed a large patch of thick fog that seemed to be resting on the ocean straight ahead. As the ship drew closer, he discerned the outline of something dark — a large mass hiding in the haze. With the fog only a few hundred feet away, Fleet realized the shape was an iceberg. He grabbed the crow's nest bell and rang it three times, then phoned the bridge.

The phone's shrill ring filled the bridge. Everyone fell silent as Sixth Officer James Moody answered. On hearing the lookout's voice Moody demanded, "What did you see?"

"Iceberg, right ahead."

Without waiting for the words to sink in, Moody thanked Fleet, hung up, and repeated the words to First Officer Murdoch.

Murdoch immediately ordered, "Full speed astern" to reverse the engines then he ordered, "Hard a-starboard," to turn the ship. With all his strength, Moody spun the wheel to the right. Around and around, Moody repeating his orders as it turned, "The helm is hard a-starboard, Sir."

Murdoch sounded the alarm and pulled the switch to close the watertight emergency doors, which separated the ship's holds. It took only a few seconds for the doors to respond, but it must have seemed like an eternity. As they waited, the steel doors separating the boiler and engine rooms slammed shut. The stokers and fireman were caught off guard and had to scramble to evacuate their stations before the doors closed them in. Some were forced to climb emergency ladders to escape.

The bridge officers stood silently, hoping against hope, but it was already too late. As the iceberg scraped along the *Titanic's* starboard side, the crew heard a horrible grinding sound resonating from somewhere deep within the ship.

Captain Smith, jarred awake by the force of the collision, rushed onto the bridge. "What was that?" he demanded.

Murdoch quickly replayed the last few minutes. Smith ordered the emergency door closed, something Murdoch assured him had already been done. But even though only a few minutes had elapsed between the lookout's warning and the crew's quick action, a huge, underwater spur protruding from the iceberg had done its damage. It scraped along the ship's side about 90 metres, exerting enough pressure to fracture the rivets that sealed the ship's almost four-centimetre-thick, double-walled, steel hull. Even with the watertight doors sealed, icy saltwater gushed into three holds and two engine rooms.

Smith ordered the engines cut and instructed the ship's carpenter to perform a thorough sounding of the ship. He then went to the wheelhouse to consult an instrument known as a "commutatorin," a device that records how level the ship is sitting in the water. It showed the great vessel was already listing five degrees to starboard.

Mary Fortune had been jarred awake by the violent shiver that ran through the ship. Millie Brown, the Allisons' new cook, was frightened by a loud grating sound, reminiscent of iron ploughing through a large pile of gravel. Further below, in the bowels of the ship, some of the third-class passengers were literally flung from their berths by the force of the crash.

Surprisingly, a number of passengers slept right through the collision. Two young women whose cabin was on B deck, close to the Baxters, told Peuchen that, had it not been for the hysterical voice of another female passenger resonating loudly through the hallway, they might have missed the whole thing.

For others, like Hélène Baxter, it wasn't the crash but

the silence afterwards that was alarming. After four days at sea the steady vibration of the engines had come to feel normal, even comforting. The sudden silence caused Hélène, who was still confined to her room, to become extremely anxious.

The men still lounging in the smoking room noticed the silencing of the engines, but most just waited, expecting an announcement to be forthcoming. It was only after some discussion that a few volunteered to investigate on deck.

Peuchen, getting ready for bed in his room, felt the ship suddenly shift to one side. "She quivered under it somewhat, like a heavy wave had just struck." Because he had recently been on deck, and had noted the unusually calm sea and the lack of wind or waves, he decided to investigate. Pulling his overcoat on over his nightshirt he headed to the upper deck.

On the Grand Staircase he encountered a casual acquaintance from his time on the ship. As they passed each other, Peuchen inquired whether the man knew what had happened. "Why, we have struck an iceberg," the man replied, urging Peuchen to go up on deck and see the chunks of ice strewn about.

Once on deck, Peuchen discovered that for a distance of 12 to 15 metres, the starboard side of the bow was covered with small chunks of soft ice, three to five centimetres thick. The ice crunched under his feet. The crisp, salty air smelled clammy, like the inside of a damp cave. For a few minutes he hung around discussing the situation with other passengers.

Some were still dressed in their evening clothes but others, like Peuchen, were already dressed for bed. He then wandered over to Hugo Ross's room to assure his sick friend that although the ship had struck an iceberg, it was nothing serious.

It wasn't long, however, before hundreds of passengers were streaming from their cabins, congregating in hallways and common areas, desperately seeking information about the accident. The stewards calmly assured them there was nothing to be concerned about. Some were reassured; some were not.

Peuchen ran in to Molson, and the two friends stood pondering the situation. About 15 minutes later, Charles Hays and his son-in-law, Thornton Davidson, came down the corridor toward them.

Peuchen extended his hand to greet the older man. "Mr. Hays," he inquired, "have you seen the ice?" Discovering he had not, Peuchen escorted them up to the forward deck. For the first time he noticed that the boat was listing dramatically toward starboard, the side on which the ship had struck the iceberg. Alarmed, he queried Charles as to why the ship would list. "She should not do that," he said. "The water is perfectly calm, and the boat has stopped."

Charles just shrugged off Peuchen's concerns, assuring him, "No matter what we have struck, she is good for eight or ten hours." This information, he said, came from one of the best old seamen. He went on to say, "Before that time comes, we will surely have assistance."

Even as Charles spoke, a design flaw in the big ship was becoming apparent. When constructing the waterproof compartments, the builder had decided to extend the wall dividers for the last five watertight chambers only as high as D deck. The middle eight dividers went only up to E deck. This meant that, as the first six compartments filled with sea water, the bow of the ship was pulled down, allowing water to easily wash over the top of the remaining watertight dividers, gradually filling each dry compartment with sea water.

As the mail room began to flood, mail clerks tried frantically to drag the letters to higher ground. The forward cargo hold and boiler rooms 5 and 6 were flooded. Within 45 minutes of the impact, the squash courts on G deck were flooded as well.

With the inspection of the ship, Captain Smith realized that his beautiful, unsinkable ship, stranded on the dark ocean some 600 kilometres off the coast of Newfoundland, was indeed sinking. Immediately, he turned his full attention to saving his passengers.

At 12:05 a.m. on Monday, Captain Smith, at the urging of First Officer Lightoller, ordered all able-bodied seamen to proceed to the forecastle of the ship to prepare the lifeboats. Each boat's cover was stripped off, and its davits unscrewed. It was then swung out over the ship's side and readied for filling and lowering. The sailors moved quickly and quietly, trying not to attract attention. To their surprise, the lifeboats moved out easily on the davits. This was a major improvement over the older davits still used on many other ships. Crew members were able to turn out all the lifeboats within 20 minutes.

Several passengers had already made their way to the top deck, but many others had taken the stewards' words to heart and gone back to their rooms, some even went to the gymnasium for a late-night workout. Hud Allison totally rejected the idea that they were in any danger, reassuring Bess that she had plenty of time to dress.

With the boats ready, the captain ordered the stewards to knock on every cabin door and tell every passenger to strap on a life belt and head to the boat deck as quickly as possible. Suddenly there were people everywhere. Caught in the surging crowd, Peuchen spotted Beattie across the room and called out to his friend, "What's the matter?"

"Why, the order is for life belts and boats," Beattie replied.

At first Peuchen didn't comprehend his friend's words. It was all so sudden. Could the situation really be that dire? But Beattie, leaving the baffled Peuchen behind, ran to wake up Hugo Ross. Meanwhile, Peuchen returned to his cabin to change into heavier, warmer clothing. He dressed quickly, grabbing his overcoat and life belt as he stepped back into the hallway. In his pocket were three oranges and a small pearl pin that he always carried for luck. He left behind his jewellery, the presents he had bought for his children, and more than $200,000 in stocks and bonds.

Danger Ahead

The ship's corridors were soon jammed with people and general confusion began to take over. Peuchen had to fight his way along the corridor through a sea of sombre passengers clad in bulky white life belts. Cabin doors opened out into the hallway, as passengers peeked out tentatively, confused and unsure of what to do. Anxious women, many crying, headed for the stairs. Some had taken the time to dress sensibly for the emergency at hand. Others had not. Down below, on the third-class level, many passengers were lost in the chaos and confusion of the moment.

Several passengers on the starboard side of the ship had witnessed the gigantic iceberg as it pushed past their portholes. Chunks of broken ice still lay on their window ledges. On the upper decks of the ship, however, there was no mass panic. Almost everyone believed the stewards' orders were only a precaution. The women, most thought, would be picked up shortly by another ship, probably the *Titanic's* sister ship, the *Olympic,* and taken to New York, while the men would remain on the *Titanic* as she was towed to Newfoundland for repair. They were confident it was an adventure that would be all over by morning.

Chapter 5
Women and Children First

With her engines disabled, the *Titanic's* gigantic boilers were forced to blow off their excess steam. This caused an ear-piercing sound, loud enough to be heard over 15 kilometres away on that clear night. The din from the boilers lasted close to three-quarters of an hour, making it virtually impossible for the officers to relay their orders to the passengers or the crew. This was compounded by the shrill whine of the rescue rockets Captain Smith had ordered to be fired every four or five minutes. The racket also made it difficult for the Marconi operators to relay their messages, but they pressed on, desperately trying to raise another ship that was close enough to help.

The first ship to answer was the *Frankfurt,* but it was

situated more than 270 kilometres away. The *Olympic,* on her way to England, also responded, but she was 800 kilometres away. She couldn't possibly get back to her sister ship until late the next evening.

Harold Cottam, the wireless operator on the Cunard Line's *Carpathia,* which was headed to the Mediterranean from New York, had already retired for the night, turning off his equipment, when he remembered the ice warning he'd planned to transmit to the *Titanic.* Restarting his equipment, he punched in the *Titanic's* call letters, MGY. Before he could even start his message, Phillips, the *Titanic's* wireless operator, cut him off. Intently, Cottam listened as the big ship's distress message made its way across the ocean: "Come at once, we have hit a berg. CQD [Come Quick Danger]," followed by the ship's coordinates: latitude 41°46' N, longitude 50°14' W.

Grabbing the message, Cottam ran with it to the bridge. Captain Roltron quickly compared the coordinates with his ship's course and determined the *Titanic* was only about 90 kilometres away. He ordered the ship turned about and another shift of stokers was sent to help feed the engines. Full speed ahead, at 15 knots, the *Carpathia* headed to the *Titanic's* aid. But it was a taxing journey, and one that would take close to three-and-a-half hours.

Peuchen was now back up on the boat deck. From where he stood he could see lifeboats ready for action, their covers removed and their ropes cleared. Passengers milled about waiting for instructions, but many soon retreated back into the warmth of the ship, away from the noise and the fiercely cold night air. For Peuchen, the gravity of the situation was finally sinking in.

Suddenly, close to a hundred coal stokers appeared on the *Titanic's* deck. Still dressed in their filthy work T-shirts, their dunnage bags slung over their shoulders, the frantic men crowded onto the deck, making it virtually impossible for anyone to move. Peuchen had never experienced such bedlam. Then, just as suddenly, an officer stepped forward and ordered the men to clear the deck and return to their stations. For a split second they appeared to hesitate then they turned and silently complied, heading back down into the bowels of the ship, most certainly to their deaths.

With the bedlam finally under control Peuchen overheard an officer say that the sails and masts had to be removed from the lifeboats. Surveying the deck, he was surprised to see very few sailors present; they were not at their stations. This seemed unusual and he wondered if the *Titanic's* crew was what a yachtsman might call a "scratch crew," made up of men hired from different vessels who were neither accustomed to working together nor knowledgeable about the ship they were on. So, when the officer turned to Peuchen, inquiring whether he might give them a hand, he willingly climbed into the dangling lifeboat to help. Using a knife he cut the lashings on the mast and sail and, with the help of another a sailor, hauled the heavy mast out of the swinging lifeboat. The boat was then slowly lowered down the side of the ship, until it was in line with the gunwale (the upper edge of the side of the ship).

The officer in charge then called for the women and children to come forward and board the lifeboat. A great many women came with their husbands, but when they were told the men could not go, they hesitated. The men urged them to go, reassuring them that they would all be back together by morning. One woman, refusing to leave without her husband, had to be pried off as he insisted that she climb into the boat. Finally she relented and climbed aboard.

* * *

There was no changing Bess Allison's mind. Sarah Daniels, Bess's maid, was the first to approach the sleeping Allisons to report the collision. She knocked on their cabin door, only to be rebuffed by Hud. But she persisted; trying everything she could think of to get her boss to take her seriously. At one point, she even grabbed his arm, but he only scolded her and ordered her back to her cabin. Finally, believing that if she were to survive she would have to fend for herself, she donned her fur-lined overcoat and headed to the boat deck, leaving Alice Cleaver to deal with baby Trevor.

On reaching the stairs, Daniels was approached by a steward who helped her put on her life belt. Still concerned about the Allisons' well-being, she enlisted his help, requesting that he go back and waken them. He agreed, and sent Daniels to the boat deck, where she boarded lifeboat 8.

Back in the cabin, Cleaver couldn't decide what to do with Trevor. Should she wake him and risk Hud's wrath? Or should she simply let him sleep? Finally a steward made the decision for her. Banging on her door he demanded that she don her life belt and head to the boat deck. She bundled up Trevor warmly, and they headed out.

It has been hinted that Cleaver possessed very little child-care experience and that she seemed awkward when handling the boy. And most people who met her would agree that she was no beauty. Her dark eyes, broad nose, and turned-down lips gave her a daunting, almost unsettling, appearance. After the accident some newspapers even went so far as to retouch her picture to make her look more appealing. It's likely that her inexperience and looks didn't help instil any sense of credibility, but then neither did the fact that her story seemed to change with each new telling.

After dressing Trevor, she said, she had gone straight to the Allisons' cabin to ensure the family was up, and to get her orders. There she found an anxious Hud, desperate to investigate what had happened. He ordered Cleaver to stay with Bess who, by this time, was almost incapacitated by fear, so Cleaver got Bess dressed and poured her a glass of brandy to calm her nerves. Then, with Bess's approval, she and Trevor had headed up to safety on the boat deck. Cleaver even said she had brushed past Hud on the way. She claimed she and

Trevor were ascending the Grand Staircase as Hud came down, but they did not speak.

However, when pressed, her story began to change. Later she said she had dressed the sleeping baby and wrapped him in a warm blanket and, after securing her life belt, had headed up the stairs with the rest of the passengers, just as the steward had ordered her to do. She swore she had passed Hud on the stairs, but in her panic had not called out to him. On reaching the boat deck she said they were immediately whisked away by an officer and put into a lifeboat. The lifeboat was lowered before she could get a message to the Allisons.

Whichever way it happened, one thing was for sure: Hud and Bess had no idea where their baby boy was. Peuchen spotted the worried couple as he was helping to ready the first lifeboats. They were frantically inquiring whether anyone had seen their son. Bess was adamant. She was not leaving the ship without Trevor. As she stood talking, a sailor seized her and forced both her and Loraine into a lifeboat. Bess quietly complied then, but as soon as his back was turned, collected her daughter and climbed out.

Soon after, Peuchen again noticed Hud, Bess, and Loraine standing in the vicinity of the lifeboats. They seemed to be surveying the people, still looking, he assumed, for Trevor. While he watched, another sailor motioned to little Loraine to come closer, but Bess, probably afraid of being separated from yet another child, grabbed her and held her tightly to her side. Peuchen's attention then turned to the next lifeboat. A short while later a passenger saw Bess, with Loraine in tow, running along the deck. Someone called out to her, saying that Hud was getting into a lifeboat on the other side of the ship. Bess and Loraine rushed to the port side.

* * *

When the *Titanic's* engines stopped, Hélène Baxter got extremely agitated and restless, demanding to know why they had stopped. Quigg tried to calm her, but to no avail, so he finally agreed to investigate. He didn't have to go very far for an answer, for just outside the Baxter's cabin door Quigg found Captain Smith and Joseph Ismay locked in an intense discussion. Interrupting, he questioned Smith about the nature of the problem. Captain Smith readily admitted to the young man that there had been an accident, but reassured him it was nothing serious, stressing that everything was fine and there was nothing to worry about. He then politely excused himself from the conversation and hurried back to the bridge. Ismay, however, didn't seem as optimistic. He quietly suggested that Quigg get his mother and sister dressed and take them to the boat deck. Quigg agreed, believing it was only a precaution.

Quigg helped the women into their life belts. They then joined other passengers on the slow walk to the boat deck. Quigg carried his mother, still weak from her bout with seasickness, up the Grand Staircase. It was a hard climb, the list of the ship tilting the stairs just enough to throw off his equilibrium and make the walk up difficult.

Eventually Quigg deposited Hélène and Zette on the boat deck across from lifeboat 6, which Peuchen had just finished preparing. He left them standing with the other women, and quietly stepped back. Hélène objected loudly. She became hysterical, insisting she would not be separated from her son. Quigg, hearing his mother's anguish, returned to her side, inquiring in French if she was okay. He tried to calm her, but again it was futile. Reaching into his pocket he extracted his silver flask and placed it in his mother's hand. Hélène immediately began lecturing her son on the evils of drinking but Quigg, accustomed to his mother's outbursts, shushed her. He bid her "Goodbye, take care," then stepped back into the crowd.

At this point Quigg may have headed back down into the ship to find his ladylove. Berthe had been lounging in her cabin on C deck when the ship struck the iceberg. She was aware of the accident, but because she had already changed for the night she was reluctant to leave her warm cabin. Suddenly a steward stepped in, grabbed her, and forced her out into the hallway with the other passengers heading up to the boat deck. Clad in satin bedroom slippers and a nightdress, and covered only by a light woollen motoring coat, she stood shivering on the deck, wondering if there was any truth to the steward's words. Deciding that she should at least go back and get her jewellery, Berthe reached out and tapped the shoulder of a lady next to her, a Mrs. Molly Brown, explaining to the Denver socialite that she was going back down to her cabin to retrieve her valuables. As she turned to leave, the "unsinkable Molly Brown," as she was later dubbed, advised Berthe to forget her money and jewellery and get into the lifeboat. The two women argued. Berthe was extremely reluctant to leave her possessions behind, but Brown persisted. And being a woman unaccustomed to losing an argument, she prevailed, convincing Berthe to get into the lifeboat. A few minutes later an officer grabbed Molly and tossed her in as well.

Seeing that Berthe was safely installed in lifeboat 6, Quigg appeared and, quickly and without explanation, introduced her to his mother and sister, asking them to take good care of her. He left, his mother perplexed as to why he wanted her to look after a complete stranger. Just as the lifeboat was about to be lowered, Berthe saw Quigg again. He was standing across the deck watching silently; for a brief moment their eyes met and with a slight nod of his head and a sly smile, Quigg bade his love farewell.

When First Officer Lightoller, the officer in charge of the port-side lifeboats, asked Captain Smith if he should put the women and children in the boats, the captain had replied "Yes, and lower away." Lightoller took this to mean only women and children, and subsequently barred all men from entering his lifeboats. As well, he prevented any ship's personnel, including stewardesses, from entering. When he could find no more women passengers willing to board he ordered a lifeboat lowered, even though it was barely half full, with only 28 passengers in a boat designed to hold 65.

In his defence, though, Lightoller still truly believed there was no danger and that the ship would never sink. What did concern him, though, were the new davits. Even though they had been tested and certified, he didn't feel confident that they would hold the weight of a fully loaded lifeboat, so he decided it would be better to lower the lifeboats partially full, rather than take a chance on losing one on the way down.

Chapter 6
Alone at Sea

As lifeboat 6, with Hélène, Zette, and Berthe aboard, started its descent toward the sea, a great commotion erupted. The women in the boat were yelling and waving their arms, trying desperately to get Lightoller's attention. Noticing the commotion, Lightoller told the sailors to halt then leaned over the side of the ship to inquire as to the problem. The quartermaster in charge of the lifeboat shouted back that there was only one sailor in his boat. How could he possibly manage such a large boat with only one seaman? But when Lightoller surveyed the deck there were no extra sailors standing about. There was no one to send. The few sailors he had were needed to prepare and lower the other boats. When he heard about the problem, Peuchen offered to help.

"Are you a seaman?" Lightoller asked.

"A yachtsman."

Desperately needing the help, Lightoller shrugged and said, "If you're sailor enough to get out on that fall [the rope on the free end of the block-and-tackle hoist used to lower the lifeboats], you can go down."

Peuchen immediately stepped forward, but Captain Smith, who'd been eavesdropping on the conversation, stopped him. Smith recognized how difficult it would be for even a seasoned sailor to get out onto the fall in the dark and lower himself into a lifeboat, especially one that was hanging almost two-and-a-half metres away from a listing ship and situated two or three decks down. Instead, he suggested that Peuchen go down to C deck and break a window close to where the lifeboat was hanging. But crawling through a broken window didn't seem feasible to Peuchen. He assured the captain that if he could just get a hold of the rope, he'd have no problem lowering himself down.

So, just three days short of his 53rd birthday, Major Peuchen reached out over the side of the tilting ship and seized the rope. With a firm grip, he swung himself out over the rail and off the ship. For a brief moment he dangled high up in the air, far above the lifeboat. Then slowly, hand over hand, he made his way down close to six metres of rope, landing safely in the waiting lifeboat.

At 12:55 a.m., with Peuchen safely aboard, lifeboat 6 resumed its slow descent toward the water. The women aboard held their breath. Some even closed their eyes, afraid to watch as they descended some 200 metres to the cold, black ocean below.

While lifeboat 6 was being lowered on the port side, lifeboats on the starboard side were also being readied. After a quick tour of the ice-strewn deck, Charles Hays went back to his cabin to wake his wife and daughter. He was still positive there was no danger, but decided it would be prudent to put the women into a lifeboat anyway.

Fifth Officer Harold Godfrey Lowe had only managed to get about 10 women into his starboard lifeboat number 3. He scoured the deck yelling, "Who's next for the boat?" Calling out for all woman and children to come, he got no response. There was a knot of people standing on the forepart of the deck, close to the gymnasium door, but as far as he could see there were no women in that group or anywhere else on the deck, so he called for any male passengers willing to go. There were 12 takers. Among them was Mr. Albert Dick, who had just finished helping his young wife, Vera, into the boat. The Dicks, who were married on May 31, 1911, the same day the *Titanic* was launched, were on their way back to Alberta, after a belated European honeymoon. Albert and his brother Bert were partners in a sawmill in Ponoka. They also dabbled in real estate, having built the Hotel Alexandra and the Dick Business Block, which still stands on 8th Street in southeast Calgary.

Even though lifeboat 3 was now also taking men, Charles

was still convinced it was all just a formality and declined to follow his wife into the boat. Instead, he and his son-in-law, Thornton Davidson, chose to wait in the warmth of the ship for rescuers to come. As they said goodbye, Charles promised Clara he would go back down to their stateroom and pack a small bag for each of them. His daughter, Orian, was so reassured by her father's calm and confident manner that she didn't even bother to kiss him or her husband goodbye.

After he had exhausted all the male volunteers from among the passengers, Lowe selected five crew members to man the boat, and gave the order to lower it. Lifeboat 3 carried only 32 people, again well short of its capacity of 65. It also contained one four-legged passenger, Sun Yat Sen, a small Pekinese who boarded clutched in the arms of her master, Henry Sleeper Harper. She was one of only four dogs to survive that night.

At first everything went smoothly. Lifeboat 3 moved slowly down toward the water, but Lowe had neglected to designate an officer in charge. Soon chaos ensued. With little or no experience in lowering lifeboats, the sailors handling the ropes couldn't seem to stay coordinated. Like a seesaw, one side pulled harder than the other and the boat's bow rose. Then, in a frantic attempt to correct the problem, the other side would over-compensate and the stern of the lifeboat would rise dramatically. The lifeboat was constantly dangling at a precarious angle, its passengers sure it would capsize at any moment and dump them into the ocean below. Back and forth, back and forth it went. Eventually, as if by some good fortune, order took over; the sailors began to work together smoothly, the boat levelled off, and gradually the lifeboat inched down. It landed quite gently in the water, its frightened passengers delighted to be down. Some, however, must have wondered if it might have been safer to stay on board.

It was now 1 a.m.

Mark Fortune always refused to travel anywhere without his prized Winnipeg Buffalo Coat. He'd brag to anyone who would listen about the ability of the heavy, matted, moth-eaten, buffalo-hide garment to keep him toasty warm in all conditions. Mary, though, had never shared his enthusiasm, and before they left Winnipeg she had begged him to leave the coat at home, stressing that there could be no possible use for it on this trip. Believing the coat to be his lucky charm, Mark had prevailed. Carefully folded up in his steamer trunk, it had lounged in comfort as they dragged it all across Europe.

Escorting his girls toward the ship's stairs, he wore it with pride, bragging to all about how warm he was going to be. However, he never got the chance to try it out. As they approached the bottom of the stairs leading to the boat deck a group of sailors stopped them. Charles and his father were told they could go no further. Mary and the girls, still not realizing there was any real danger, removed their jewellery and gave it to Charles for safekeeping. Then, after extracting a promise from Charles to look after their father, the women headed up the stairs to the boat deck. They, too, neglected to say goodbye.

The Fortune girls stood on the tilting deck, waiting patiently with the other women for port-side lifeboat 10 to be readied. It was cold and noisy, and soon Ethel decided it was all a waste of time. Leaving the others on deck, she returned to the warmth of her cabin.

The slant of the deck was becoming more pronounced, making it increasingly difficult to get anyone into the port-side lifeboats. The ever-growing starboard lean had widened the gap between the lifeboats and the side of the ship. The space had now grown to almost three-quarters of a metre, forcing the Fortune girls and the other women on the deck to leap over the dark void in order to get into the lifeboat. Those women who hesitated were thrown bodily, as were the children. Sailors in the lifeboats caught them by their clothing and yanked them in.

As one young lady in a black dress attempted to jump, her foot got tangled in the ship's rail. This sent her flying forward, causing her to lose her balance and fall head-first, down between the lifeboat and the ship. As she plunged over the side, Stewart William Burke grabbed her ankle and hung on with all his might. For what would have seemed like an eternity, she dangled head-first over the side of the ship. Suddenly, hands reached out from the open promenade window below and grabbed her by the shoulders. For a moment she hung suspended, one man holding her ankle and another her shoulders, until Burke let go. She fell forward and was pulled through the open window back into the ship. A few minutes later she was back up on deck ready to try again. This time she made the jump.

With no more women visible on deck, the order was given to lower lifeboat 10, the last port-side boat to be let down. Just as it started its descent, Ethel Fortune burst back on the scene. Apparently a steward had found her lounging in her room and informed her that her mother was about to enter a lifeboat. He then escorted her back up to the boat deck. By this time, the lifeboat was already disappearing over the side of the ship. Ethel was forced to jump. Somehow she made it across the void and into the lifeboat.

Not long after, just as the lifeboat was about to hit the water, a young man flung himself over the ship's rail. He landed hard in the bottom of the boat, hitting a woman and badly bruising her leg. He was Neshan Krekorian, a 25-year-old Turkish immigrant on his way to Brantford, Ontario.

It was now 1:20 a.m.

The ship's growing list was becoming a problem on the starboard side as well. The angle of the ship caused the lifeboats to dangle half over the deck and to rub against the ship as they were lowered. By the time the officers got to lifeboat 11, the list was so dramatic that they decided to lower it down to A deck and then pass the women through one of the promenade's windows. Alice Cleaver, with little Trevor

Allison, had been patiently waiting for a spot in one of the boats. When the order came for women to climb down to A deck, Cleaver obeyed. This change in plans probably sealed Bess Allison's fate.

Once down on A deck, Cleaver passed Trevor through the window, climbed aboard the lifeboat, and reclaimed her charge. Lifeboat 11, like all the emergency boats, had a capacity of 65 passengers. It now held 70. Slowly it inched its way down toward the water, scraping along the side of the ship as it went, but as it reached the ship's condenser exhaust port, the force of the escaping water almost capsized it. Only the quick thinking of the crew, who used their oars to hold the lifeboat away from the side of the ship and the condenser port, saved it. As they hit the water, they were again forced to use their oars to keep the stern of the lifeboat away from the discharging water. While the others steadied her, one of the sailors frantically sliced at the ropes securing the lifeboat to the ship. Finally, they gave way.

It was 1:45 a.m.

Chapter 7
Power Struggle

Before lifeboat 6 even hit the water the power struggle began. Immediately upon reaching the lifeboat, Peuchen inquired of the quartermaster manning the rudder whether there was anything he could do to help. "Get down and put in the plug," was the reply, so Peuchen groped along the bottom of the lifeboat among the tangle of legs, trying to find the hole. In the crowded darkness it was virtually impossible to see. Peuchen felt around with his hands but got nowhere. Finally, in desperation, he suggested that Quartermaster Hichen put in the plug, assuming he would probably have a better idea of where to look. While the quartermaster searched, Peuchen worked to undo the shackles and release the lifeboat from its rigging. With the boat finally free of the *Titanic*, Peuchen took hold of the rudder, but the quartermaster quickly overruled him, sending Peuchen forward to the port-side oar. The lone sailor in the boat, Fredrick Fleet, the lookout who had first spotted the iceberg, took the starboard oar.

As Peuchen took his place at the oar, Quartermaster Hichen started yelling at the men to row faster, screaming over and over again that the boat was going to founder. At first, Peuchen thought it was the lifeboat he was worried about, assuming that Hichen had been unable to find the hole or insert the plug properly. But the plug was not the problem. It was the *Titanic* that concerned Hichen. He believed the huge boat was about to founder and, in its wake, take them down with it. Peuchen and Fleet started pulling on the oars with all their might.

A few minutes later they heard a high-pitched whistle. They stopped rowing to listen. It was the shrill sound of an officer's whistle beckoning them to come back to the ship. Peuchen and the others wanted to row back, but Hichen refused to allow it. The women pleaded with him, but he maintained, "It is our lives now, not theirs," and ordered the men to continue rowing away.

Then Hichen noticed a light far off in the distance, and decided it must be a ship sitting just over the horizon. He ordered the men to pull toward the light. Peuchen, who was accustomed to being on the ocean at night, was sceptical, and attempted to explain to Hichen that it was probably only a reflection, an illusion of sorts. The quartermaster refused to listen. He resolved that, if it wasn't a ship, then it must be a buoy. He even called out to one of the other lifeboats, asking them if they could see the buoy. Peuchen was flabbergasted. Did this man, a quartermaster by trade, honestly believe there were buoys just floating around in the middle of the ocean?

But a good soldier follows orders and Peuchen was a good soldier, so he obeyed. Furthermore, Hichen controlled the rudder and there were a lot of women between him and Hichen, leaving Peuchen in no position to take the rudder away from the quartermaster. So he kept on rowing, rowing toward the imaginary light from the phantom mid-ocean buoy.

Rowers in lifeboat 3, with Clara and Orian on board, were also trying to get away from the *Titanic's* starboard side, but were making very little progress. Its crew members were so green that the boat soon got turned about, heading back toward the ship. George Alfred Moore, the officer in charge, was faithfully following orders when he ordered his men to row clear of the ship, but he wasn't pushing them very hard. Unlike Hichen, Moore still believed it was all just precautionary. If it had been up to him, he would have stayed on board the ship where it was dry and warm. It was only after they had managed to put a considerable distance between his lifeboat and the *Titanic* that he noticed how far down the head of the great ship had sunk. It was now lying so low in the water that waves were threatening to wash over its name.

With lifeboat 11 cut free of the *Titanic,* her sailors

attempted to pull away from the cascade of gushing water exiting the condenser port. But with 70 people crammed into a lifeboat made for 65 it was virtually impossible. The boat was so jammed that, as the men pulled back on their oars, the oar handles struck the other passengers. Cleaver held Trevor tightly, huddling against the other women as they tried to keep their feet up out of the water now sluicing about in the bottom of the boat.

Eventually lifeboat 11 was able to move about 30 metres away from the ship, and from that vantage point they could see people huddled together along the *Titanic's* rail. Parts of the ship were now sitting almost as low in the water as the lifeboats but, surprisingly, they could still hear the ship's band. Its melodies were interrupted only by the occasional hiss of rescue rockets, their brilliantly coloured sparks, like fireworks at a county fair, raining down from the sky.

By 2:05 a.m. the rockets were exhausted and all the *Titanic's* 16 standard lifeboats had been lowered safely into the water. The ship's forward upper deck was now almost completely submerged. Her gigantic propellers were lifted almost completely out of the water. Those passengers still on board were throwing barrels, chairs, and anything else that would float into the water. Some jumped and attempted to swim away, frightened that the ship's suction would pull them down. Harry Molson was up on deck, his shoes and socks removed, probably preparing for another long swim. The Allisons were still frantically searching for Trevor.

Phillips sent his last message: "Sinking by the head, have cleared boats and filled them with women and children." It was received by the *Carpathia,* but when Evans tried to reply, he was met with dead air.

The water was now only about a metre down from the main boat deck and the *Titanic's* remaining crew members were frantically trying to get the four collapsibles off the ship. Collapsibles C and D were slid over to the now empty davits, loaded, and lowered down without any problems. However, they found it virtually impossible to move collapsible A, which had been stowed on the roof of the officers' quarters. Even with its canvas sides down, it was much too heavy and awkward for the men to handle. Someone suggested they lean oars against the wall of the building and slide the lifeboat down on them, but the boat was too heavy, and the oars snapped under the weight. The collapsible toppled down to the deck below. It landed upright, but the fall crippled the mechanism that raised its canvas sides. Suddenly a shudder ran through the ship as a large wave washed over her bow. Many of the men helping move the collapsibles were washed out into the sea. Worried that time had run out, a sailor cut the ropes attaching collapsible A to the ship. Just then another wave hit, taking collapsible A and the remaining sailors with it as it retreated back to the sea.

The collapsible landed upright on the surface of the ocean, with its sides still down, but fortunately it floated. Several people swam over to the raft-like platform and pulled themselves aboard. Beattie and McCaffry, who had been seen standing together on the deck earlier, must have been close to the collapsible when it was forced into the water. Beattie managed to get himself up onto the boat. He was wet, cold, and alone but, for the time being, safe.

Back on the ship, there was a loud explosion. To Peuchen it sounded like a sharp rumble. It was followed by a popping, cracking sound, then by a second explosion. The great ship's lights dimmed and flickered. A moment later, they went out for good. Only the faint glow of the lantern hanging from the mast remained. Peuchen turned and glanced back at what was left of the magnificent ship. It was now very dark and he was too far away to see anything clearly, but for a moment he thought he saw the outlines of people standing along her rail.

Someone in lifeboat 3 yelled, "She's gone, lads! Row like hell or we'll get the devil of a swell." As if on cue, the great ship rose up out of the water, her stern arcing toward the sky. For a split second, people hung from her rails. Then the ship emitted a loud, metallic, ripping sound. Gases emerged from her funnels and red-hot sparks shot into the air. Some observers later swore that she went down in one piece. In reality she broke in two, snapping between her third and fourth funnels. Almost immediately, her bow headed straight down to the ocean floor, more than three kilometres below. Her stern rose up out of the water as though pulled by some invisible cable, its vastness outlined against the night sky, as if it were suspended between life and death. Then, like a dagger piercing the surface of the dark, cold water, the last of the ship disappeared forever from the eyes of her horrified audience.

The lifeboats were now at least half a kilometre away from where the *Titanic* went down, but survivors could still hear the cries of the dying — the dreadful sound of people thrashing about in cold water, desperately trying to save themselves until, with their energy sapped, they slowly surrendered to hypothermia. It was a sound most would never forget.

Ethel Fortune swore that she saw her brother, Charles, floundering about among the rubble. She recalled him struggling in the water, with only his life belt to keep him afloat. However, likely it was just her mind playing tricks. The night was much too dark, and their lifeboat much too far away, for her to have seen anything clearly. Logic did not make the image, which remained in her mind, any less real. It created a vivid portrait of her dying brother, one that haunted her for the rest of her life.

The women in Peuchen's boat started begging Hichen again to go back. Now that the ship was gone, they reasoned, there was no danger of them being sucked down in its wake. But again he refused, explaining that it was useless as "there were only a lot of stiffs left." The women were horrified. How could he talk about their loved ones that way? They badgered him. Hélène cried out for her son, but Hichen refused to budge. Peuchen was also horrified by the quartermaster's remarks, but he had by then realized that it was useless to try to reason with this man.

Mercifully for those in the water, hypothermia set in quickly and soon their cries subsided. With the *Titanic* gone, the water was again perfectly calm. The dark, frigid sea seemed to stretch out forever around the lonesome lifeboats. Their only light now came from a sky full of twinkling stars and the lifeboat lanterns. It was dead quiet.

Chapter 8
One Long, Dark Night

CQD ... CQD ... crackled through the wireless set at Cape Race, Newfoundland. The lighthouse, resting on the southern tip of the Avalon Peninsula, was accustomed to relaying messages from passing ships, but this one was different. The frantic CQD was coming from a passenger ship about 600 kilometres southeast of Cape Race — a ship called the *Titanic*.

At about the same time that Cape Race received the *Titanic's* message, George Hannah, the traffic manager at the Allan Steamship Company in Montreal, received an urgent request from one of his company's ships, the *Virginian*. Two days out of Halifax on its way to Liverpool with a hull full of perishable apples, she was requesting permission to deviate from her course and assist an ailing ship some 270 kilometres distant.

The credo of the sea avows that any ship always comes to the aid of another, so Hannah gave his consent. As the *Virginian* made a wide, arcing turn, Hannah called his friend Edward Stranger, a marine reporter with the *Montreal Gazette*. Stranger, excited by the prospect of news, raced up the street to the steamship offices, where the two men sat huddled over the wireless, eavesdropping on the messages flying between the ships and the Cape Race lighthouse. Stranger became the first reporter in the world to hear of the *Titanic's* plight.

Robert Hunston, one of the Cape Race operators on duty that night, recorded the exchange in his log.

10:25 p.m. (EST) [12:15 a.m. Titanic time] – J.C.R. Goodwin on watch hears Titanic *calling CQD giving position 41.44 N 50.24 W about 380 miles [612 kilometres] SSE of Cape Race.*

10:35 p.m. [12:35 a.m. Titanic time] Titanic *gives corrected position as 41.46 N 50.14 W. A matter of five or six miles difference [eight or nine kilometres]. He says, "Have struck iceberg."*

10:40 p.m. [12:40 a.m. Titanic time] Titanic *calls* Carpathia *and says, "We require immediate assistance." Gray on duty.*

10:55 p.m. [12:55 a.m. *Titanic* time] Titanic *tells German steamer, "Have struck iceberg and sinking."*

11:00 p.m. [1:00 a.m. *Titanic* time] Titanic *continues calling for assistance and giving position.*

11:36 p.m. [1:36 a.m. *Titanic* time] Olympic *asks* Titanic *which way latter steering.* Titanic *replies, "We are putting women off in boats."*

12:50 a.m. [2:50 a.m. *Titanic* time] Virginian *says last he heard of* Titanic *was at 12:27 a.m.* [2:27 a.m. *Titanic* time] *when latter signals were blurred and ended abruptly.*

It was 1:40 a.m. on Monday before the New York papers got wind of the accident. A reporter from the Associated Press immediately called Philips Frankland, vice-president of the White Star Line. Awakened from a deep sleep, Frankland refused to comment, but minutes later, at his New York office, Frankland's worst fears were confirmed. Almost immediately, every major newspaper on two continents was onto the story. It was a media free-for-all. Radio wavelengths everywhere were jammed. Hunston estimated that, that morning alone, Cape Race was deluged with close to 300 messages, mostly from newspapers.

Back out on the Atlantic, Peuchen and the fleet were getting weary. They'd been rowing constantly since the lifeboat hit the water. Many of the women had also taken turns pulling one or the other of the oars, but Quartermaster Hichen had stubbornly refused to leave the rudder. The sea was still perfectly calm and there was nothing nearby for them to hit, except maybe another lifeboat, so Peuchen suggested that one of the women hold the rudder while Hichen take his turn at the oar. Again the quartermaster refused, ordering Peuchen to row harder, to row toward the light that only Hichen could see. He wildly criticized the men for not rowing properly, for not holding their oars at the right angle, for not rowing fast enough.

For much of the time before the *Titanic* sank, Hichen had been badgering the women about how they would be sucked down and lost when the big ship went under, repeatedly reminding them of the force she had exerted on the *New York* and assuring them that, even if by some quirk of fate the ship didn't pull them down with her, her boilers would get them. As the giant boilers settled to the sea bottom, he explained, they would explode, unleashing a massive wave that would tear apart the icebergs and swamp their tiny lifeboats.

However, the *Titanic* had gone to her final grave quietly, without taking any lifeboats with her. In fact, she had barely made a ripple. So Hichen was forced to change his tune. From his perch high up above the rudder he now lectured the women, including Hélène, Zette, and Berthe, about the evils of the sea, using words more suited to a barroom brawl than to mixed company. He battered the frightened women with his vision of the future, constantly reminding them that they were hundreds of kilometres away from the closest land or assistance, bobbing about alone in the middle of the ocean, without food or drinking water. He described how they would drift for days, and how cold the nights would be.

It was all too much for Hélène, who sat sobbing, often uncontrollably, but Hichen didn't seem to notice the effect he was having on the women. Or maybe he just didn't care. He pressed on. Did they not know they were sitting ducks, just waiting for a cruel Atlantic storm to do them in? Had they not heard of the horrors of starvation or the terrors of drowning? He reminded them that, without a compass or any landmarks to rely upon, they had no hope of finding their way. At one point one of the ladies interrupted him and, pointing to the North Star, suggested they could use it to navigate. Hichen disregarded her logic and picked up his rant where he had left off. Peuchen attempted to intercede, begging Hichen to quiet down, and to tone down his language for the sake of the ladies. Hichen didn't see a need to clean up his act. Instead, he again put Peuchen in his place, reminding him who was boss.

Finally, Molly Brown snapped. She had had enough of Hichen's nonsense. She openly chastised him for his cruelty and laziness. In return she got a volley of cuss words, but

Molly was not one to back down. She kept at him, ordering him to stop. They argued, their angry words flying back and forth. Finally, Molly threatened to throw Hichen overboard. He must have believed she would do it, because for a while he was quiet.

His attention now turned to Hélène and the silver flask she was holding. He demanded she pass it over. Hélène refused. She had spent most of the night sobbing, repeating Quigg's name over and over again, and she was not likely to part with her only remaining connection to her son. Again, Hichen didn't seem to care. They quarrelled, neither willing to budge from their position. Finally, to appease him, Hélène agreed to give him her extra steamer blanket. Hichen took it and left all of the women alone for a while.

Lifeboat 16 was now very close to number 6, so the officers in charge decided to tie the two boats together for a while. But the sea had begun to get choppy, and as they tried to bring the two lifeboats closer, they crashed into each other. Peuchen suggested that they hang life belts over the side between the boats, to act as a cushion. His plan worked, and with the two lifeboats now securely tied together, bobbing freely with the current, at last Peuchen could rest.

A new day was emerging and the morning light revealed to the lifeboat passengers the cluster of towering icebergs that encircled them. It was as though they were resting in a nest of bergs. Peuchen counted five large icebergs and at least two smaller ones. Some were jagged. Some were smooth. Two stood at least 30 metres high, their footprint over 100 metres wide. They towered over the lifeboats like giant, floating islands.

By now most of the survivors had been awake for close to 24 hours. They were cold and tired. Many, like the three Fortune girls, had blisters on their hands from rowing. Now that it was light, Fifth Officer Lowe, who was in charge of lifeboat 14, decided to round up some of the lifeboats and tie them together. He herded up five lifeboats, including lifeboat 10 with the Fortune women on board. Once they were securely tied he distributed his passengers among the other boats. He then rigged his sail and, taking advantage of the growing breeze, headed back to the area where the *Titanic* had gone down to search for survivors.

The going was slow. They had to push their way through water almost solid with bodies. At first the task seemed futile, but they persisted and eventually managed to find four survivors. A young Japanese man tied to one of the ship's doors came floating by. At first Lowe presumed he was dead, but closer examination proved he was only unconscious. They untied him and dragged him into their boat. He recovered quickly, and was even able to help them row the lifeboat after a short time.

In the distance Lowe spotted a collapsible floating upside down, its bottom lined with men all clinging precariously to the raft and to one another. They quickly rowed over and, after tying their boat to collapsible B, carefully transferred the cold, weary men one by one into their little flotilla. Then Lowe spotted another collapsible. This one was upright, with its canvas sides down. Its passengers had spent the whole night sitting in 30 centimetres of water. They made their way over to collapsible A, in the hope of saving the twenty men and one woman who clung to its deck.

Not everyone would be saved. As the sun rose that morning, Olaus Abelseth, a 25-year-old, third-class passenger who had managed to pull himself aboard the sideless collapsible shortly after the *Titanic* had sunk, noticed that his neighbour was in grave distress. The man, still dressed in evening clothes, was slumped over on the deck of the collapsible. Abelseth grabbed him by the shoulders and tried to raise him up. He shook him, shouting and begging him to hang on, saying, "We can see a ship now! Brace up!" He then raised the man's arm in the air, but the man was much too tired to care, "Who are you?" he mumbled. "Who are you? Let me be."

Abelseth held him and tried to warm him, but he quickly became tired and was forced to let the man go. Grabbing a small chunk of wood from the water, he placed it under the man's head. Half an hour later he realized that the man was dead.

During the U.S. inquiry into the disaster Abelseth stated that the man he had tried to save was from New Jersey. But there was no record of a man from New Jersey ever having been on collapsible A. Instead, most researchers agree that the man Abelseth tried to save was Thomas Beattie.

Once all of collapsible A's passengers were safely transferred to his boat, Lowe inquired about the three men still lying there, asking, "Are you sure they are dead?" The other survivors were positive, so the three men were left on the crippled lifeboat, their faces discreetly covered with their life belts.

Clara Hays and her daughter, Orian, were both frozen, but they tried to put on a brave face. They had spent the night huddled together with the other women in lifeboat 3, using their life belts to shield themselves from the wind. Like most of the lifeboats, theirs had no lantern, food, or water. And the bitter cold had taken two of their oars when the men's hands had become too cold to hold on to them. Everyone was trying their best not to give up. Then suddenly, over the horizon, they spotted a faint line. It was a single red and black smoke stack off in the distance, their first glimpse of hope steaming toward them.

Chapter 9
The *Carpathia*

Upon receiving the *Titanic*'s wireless message, Captain Rostron quickly summoned his chief engineer and began preparations for the rescue mission. The first task was to turn the ship about. He charted their location and set a new course of north 52 degrees west true 58 miles from the *Carpathia*'s present position.

The *Carpathia* was only about 90 kilometres away from the *Titanic* but she faced a lengthy journey. Five large icebergs and numerous ice floes rested in the waters between the two boats, making progress agonizingly slow. Captain Rostron guided his ship gingerly through the ice floes, skirting the bergs. *Carpathia*'s 750 passengers remained unaware of the *Titanic* disaster.

Two additional lookouts were posted at the ship's bow and Second Officer James Bisset was ordered to stand watch. He took up his post on the *Carpathia's* starboard bridge wing, the bitter sea air numbing his cheeks. Captain Rostron ordered all hands on deck. Some were to prepare the lifeboats, others readied the ship to receive survivors.

The ship's three doctors set up makeshift hospitals in the dining rooms — the English doctor in first class, the Italian doctor in second class, and the Hungarian doctor in the third-class dining room. Each was instructed to prepare the supplies necessary for any kind of emergency.

Stewards headed to the kitchen to help prepare coffee, soup, and other hot drinks. Sentinels were situated in the hallways to intercept and calm any of *Carpathia's* passengers who might awaken. Blankets were collected, and every usable space on the ship, including the smoking room and library, was turned into makeshift accommodation. Captain Rostron and his officers even vacated their cabins to make room for survivors.

Like most big ships of her time, the *Carpathia* wasn't built to quickly and easily retrieve people from the ocean, so her crew scoured the ship looking for anything that might help them pluck survivors from the water. They quickly amassed a small collection of boatswain's sling chairs, ropes, Jacob's ladders, and canvas ash bags, in which they could hoist small children onto the ship. Heaving lines were distributed along the side of the ship to secure incoming lifeboats. Rostron ordered the ship's rockets to be fired every 15 minutes, in the hope that the *Titanic* would see and hear them coming. He then retreated to the bridge, where he was observed standing alone with his head bowed in silent prayer.

For the rest of the journey Captain Rostron remained on the bridge, squinting into the distance, searching for any sign of the gigantic ship. At one point he spotted a faint green glow which he mistook for the lights of the *Titanic* and for a brief moment he was ecstatic, believing that they had made it in time. But as they drew closer to the co-ordinates given in the *Titanic*'s final transmission, the joy of Captain Rostron and his crew quickly waned. Their anxious eyes discerned only water, ice, and a few small lifeboats for as far as they could see.

The women in lifeboat 6 spotted the *Carpathia*'s rockets long before they spotted her funnel. Excitedly they pointed out the bright bursts of light. Quartermaster Hichen, although quieter and much better behaved after Molly's threat, discounted their sighting, dismissing it as the light from a falling star. Even with the *Carpathia* in full view, Hichen still refused to allow the boats to be untied, declaring the ship was not there to rescue them, but only to retrieve bodies.

Survivors were overjoyed at the sight of the *Carpathia*. Some cried, some cheered, but many just sat there, as if frozen in time, too cold and tired to move. However, as the ship got closer, the joy of many turned to worry. Would those on board the approaching ship notice their tiny boats bobbing in the water? Or would she unknowingly pass by without seeing them or, worse yet, run right over them?

In a desperate attempt to get her attention they began burning matches, paper, or anything flammable they could find. When the occupants of lifeboat 3 ran out of paper Orian removed her straw hat, set it aflame, and waved it high in the air. The ship was now getting closer, and, to the survivors' delight, it seemed to be stopping. Soon the *Carpathia* was so close that the survivors could see people moving about on deck. Relieved, their pent-up tears of joy and sorrow flowed freely.

The *Carpathia* was no *Titanic*. At 13,600 tons she was only about a quarter of the size of the mammoth liner they had just lost. Still, in the early morning light she looked safe, warm, and exceedingly inviting to the cold, tired survivors. Frantically, they untied their little huddle of lifeboats, and, with a surge of renewed energy, each crew rowed toward the waiting ship. Hichen finally agreed to untie lifeboat 6, but only after he was commanded to do so by Molly Brown.

At 4:10 a.m. the first lifeboat pulled up to the *Carpathia's* open gangway door. By the time it was secured the swell had changed. Small, choppy waves tossed the little lifeboat to and fro, grinding it against the side of the ship.

Clara, Orian, and the other women made their way over to the bottom of the Jacob's ladders hanging over the side of the ship. It was a difficult climb. Many balked at first, doubting they could make it up since, by this time, their hands were so cold they could barely hold the rope. All were eventually persuaded to make the effort. As a precaution, ropes were tied around the women's waists to catch them in case they slipped. One woman did slip; she dangled at the end of her rope, swinging along the side of the ship for a few terrifying minutes until she regained her grip on the ladder.

Loraine Allison's little friend Robert Spedden, the only child in lifeboat 3, was hoisted up in an ash bag. Women not strong enough to climb were pulled up on boatswain's chairs.

Lifeboat 11 tied up to the *Carpathia.* The Fortune girls, their blistered hands still stinging, now tackled the long rope ladders. As each lifeboat emptied, *Carpathia*'s deck became more and more crowded. Most of the survivors were suffering from exposure; they had spent almost seven hours floating in unheated lifeboats on the cold Atlantic Ocean. The three doctors assessed their new patients rapidly, filling the makeshift hospitals with people who suffered from broken bones or swollen feet, or who were just too cold or disoriented to walk. Those able to walk unaided were wrapped in warm blankets, escorted below deck to warm up, and given hot, comforting drinks. Many of the women refused to go below. They stood on deck, pressed up against the rail, hoping the next lifeboat would return a loved one to them. Each one kept her own silent vigil, but most were disappointed. The grief of these women, newly widowed, was heartbreaking.

With all the fighting and quarrelling going on over the untying of the ropes, Major Peuchen's lifeboat was one of the last to reach the *Carpathia*. By that time the ocean had become extremely choppy and it took three or four attempts before they were able to dock safely. Each time they tried, the lifeboat was dashed against the keel of the ship. Eventually they managed to tie up and get their passengers on board the *Carpathia*.

The first thing Zette Douglas did when she boarded the *Carpathia* was to cable her husband, Dr. Frederick Douglas, in Montreal. The cable read, "Meet steamer *Carpathia*, Cunard Line, Thursday, New York with James" (her eldest brother). Shortly after, she attempted to send another message, this time telling Frederick they were safe and asking him to wire them if he heard anything from Quigg. But the wireless operator was so swamped that her second message was never sent. Hélène, still in a bewildered state at the loss of her beloved son, Quigg, stumbled around as if in a daze, teetering on the verge of hysterics. Many other women wandered the deck in a similar state.

With all the lifeboats emptied, the crew began the gruelling task of retrieving the boats from the water and stowing them on deck. Just as they were finishing this task, the Leyland liner the *Californian* arrived on the scene.

The *Californian*, on its way to Boston, had also encountered ice the previous evening. Its captain, Stanley Lord, decided it was much too dangerous to proceed, and ordered his crew to halt the ship for the night. A few minutes before 11 p.m., the *Californian's* wireless operator, Cyril Evans, had radioed the *Titanic* to advise her they had stopped and were preparing to sit it out until morning. It was at this time that *Titanic* wireless operator Phillips, still frantically trying to catch up on his messages, had cut Evans off so abruptly. Evans was tired, and did not relish the idea of getting into an argument with another wireless operator, so he'd decided to call it a night. He turned off his wireless set and went to bed.

Later that night the *Californian's* night crew had noticed a large passenger liner stopped some 10 to 15 kilometres south of them. Shortly after midnight the ship started firing rockets. They notified Captain Lord, but the assumption was that the ship, like theirs, must have stopped for the night and was throwing a party. By 2:20 a.m. the ship had disappeared. The *Californian's* crew assumed it had simply steamed off. For the rest of the night the *Californian* bobbed lazily on the ocean, probably only a few kilometres away from where the *Titanic* had sunk.

By 6 a.m. on Monday, when Evans powered up his wireless equipment, the airwaves were jammed with news of the *Titanic*. Captain Lord ordered his ship to head for the *Titanic's* last known location. By 6:30 p.m. they had cleared the thickest parts of the ice field and were proceeding at full speed toward the place where the *Titanic* had sunk. At 8:30 p.m. they pull up alongside the *Carpathia*.

Chapter 10
Heading Home

After a short discussion the captains of the two ships agreed that the *Californian* would stay behind and look for survivors amidst the wreckage, while the *Carpathia* took her collection of battered survivors back to New York. The *Carpathia's* engines were started, and her crew readied her for the long trip back.

Before leaving, Captain Rostron decided it would be appropriate to organize two short services, one in thanksgiving for the 705 passengers safely aboard his ship, the second in remembrance of the approximately 1,500 others who were still unaccounted for. At the appointed time hundreds of survivors crowded the deck. An Episcopal clergyman who was travelling on the *Carpathia* officiated. The mood was sombre. The crowd, mostly women, stood quietly as the clergyman spoke. They didn't want to believe so many others had perished.

While the service was being conducted Captain Rostron slowly manoeuvred the ship through the wreckage. He scanned the water carefully but, to his surprise, saw only one body. It was that of a man, probably a *Titanic* crew member. He was lying on his side, with his head flopped back and his life belt holding his torso out of the water. There was no mistake, though, he was definitely dead. Hoping to spare the assembled passengers further trauma, and to avoid unnecessary hysteria, Rostron did not attempt to recover the body, but let the *Carpathia* steam quietly past.

Peuchen was also up on the deck, keenly scanning the ocean below. The water seemed to be littered with cork. Peuchen assumed it was from the life belts, but it was actually insulation from the *Titanic's* hull. A barbershop pole floated by, leaving Peuchen to wonder what kind of explosion would rip such a well-secured pole from its moorings.

He later reflected:

> *When we steamed through this wreckage, after we left the scene of the disaster, I was interested to see if I could see any bodies, and I was surprised to think that with all these deaths that had taken place we could not see one body; ...*
>
> *I understand a life preserver is supposed to keep up a person, whether dead or alive ...*

*Because there was a breeze started up at day-
break, the wreckage would naturally float away
from where she went down, somewhat. It might be
that it had floated away, probably a mile or half a
mile; probably not more than that, considering that
the wind only sprang up at daybreak.*

The *Carpathia* began her journey to New York at about
9 a.m. It would not be an easy trip. Almost immediately she
encountered thick sheets of ice covering most of the ocean
in front of her. Slowly, she steamed parallel to the floes,
dodging icebergs as she went. After she cleared the ice, they
were treated to a violent thunderstorm followed by almost
three days of fog, with the ship's foghorn bellowing continu-
ously. The foreboding sound further unravelled the survivors'
already frayed nerves.

The *Carpathia*'s barbershop opened its doors to supply survivors with toiletry items such as toothbrushes. But
the greatest need for most survivors was warm clothing. The
lucky ones were still in their evening gowns; others wore only
their nightclothes. *Carpathia*'s passengers opened up their
hearts and their steamer trunks, offering their clothes to the
survivors. Others converted sugar sacks into clothing for the
children.

Morning in New York brought total confusion.
Speculation abounded. The *Christian Science Monitor*, out of
Boston, Massachusetts, reported "Passengers Safely Moved

and Steamer *Titanic* Taken in Tow." By April 16, the *Daily Mail* in London, England, was reporting that the *Titanic* had sunk, but with "No Lives Lost." The *Montreal Gazette* countered this report, claiming the ship was in danger, but still afloat.

Hundreds of rumours floated around. One was that the *Titanic* was on her way to Newfoundland. It was also thought that her passengers had been picked up by a number of different ships. That rumour persisted until 11:30 a.m. on Tuesday, when newspapers released a message from the captain of the *Olympic,* passed on by the Cape Race station, which read: "Please allay rumours that the *Virginia* has any *Titanic* passengers. Neither has the *Parisian.* I believe that the only survivors are on the *Carpathia.* The second, third, and fourth officers and the second Marconi operator are the only officers reported saved."

Montreal and Toronto were abuzz with excitement. Twice (once in an unverified dispatch from London), Charles Hays was reported saved. Later it was said that he had been rescued by an unnamed ship, along with novelist Jacques Futrells, and that they were headed for London.

Many speculated that the *Carpathia* was heading for Newfoundland. And, for a while at least, that was a distinct possibility. With the ship being so close to Halifax, Captain Rostron had originally contemplated docking there. After much deliberation, including discussions with the White Star Line's Joseph Ismay, it was decided to take the survivors straight to New York. This, the captain hoped, would keep the

Carpathia away from the numerous icebergs and ice floes along the Canadian coast, and save survivors from having to arrange alternate transportation to New York.

The families of *Titanic's* passengers were already starting to head to New York in anticipation of the *Carpathia's* arrival. Having received Zette's message, Dr. Douglas left his Montreal eye clinic and, with brother-in-law James in tow, raced to New York. The Grand Trunk Railway immediately dispatched their vice-president, Mr. Ross Kelly. With him were Mr. and Mrs. Hope Scott, Charles and Clara's daughter and son-in-law. They left Montreal's Bonaventure station at 7:15 a.m. on April 16.

Mrs. Heber C. Hutton, Mark Fortune's oldest daughter, travelled with her family from British Columbia. Edith Graham, the wife of T. Eaton buyer George Graham, received her husband's telegram, which she mistook for one sent after the disaster; on the assumption that he was safe, a company representative was dispatched to meet him.

New York authorities brought in additional police to maintain order around the docks and the offices of the White Star Line. They struggled to keep traffic moving as a constant procession of automobiles made its way toward the wharf. Thousands of people lined the streets, scanning the bulletins and waiting for news. The White Star Line office was bombarded with inquiries from passengers, and friends, and family of the *Titanic's* passengers.

As the *Carpathia* approached New York harbour it was

surrounded by yachts and small pleasure boats. Most had been commissioned by newspapers in an attempt to get information about the *Titanic*. The sky was peppered with camera flashes. Small boats jockeyed for position around the *Carpathia*, with reporters yelling questions at the survivors on board. Thirty thousand people, mostly just spectators, lined the streets.

Police blocked off the area around Pier 54, the same dock from which the *Carpathia* had departed only eight days earlier. The Fourteenth Street area was also cordoned off as far east as Eighth Avenue. New York Mayor William Jay Gaynor ordered 150 foot-patrolmen, 12 mounted police, and 25 detectives to man the barricades. Close to a thousand friends and family members of *Titanic* passengers huddled under the pier shed, trying desperately to keep out of the rain. They stood quietly, seemingly dumfounded by the circus swirling around them.

Hospital workers from St. Luke's and St. Vincent's, clad in their white uniforms, stood by with stretchers and wheelchairs. As the *Carpathia* docked, a squad of doctors and coroner's representatives boarded. The crowd had to wait, but not for long.

As the survivors began to disembark, the crowd grew silent. Even the camera flashes stopped.

Zette, Hélène, and Berthe came ashore together. Zette dodged the insensitive questions of the press in an attempt to protect her mother and salvage what was left of their family dignity. They introduced Berthe as a penniless widow whom the Baxters were adopting, taking her back to Montreal with them where they would care for her until she could gather the resources to return to Europe.

Hud Allison's brothers, George and Percy, were among those in the growing crowd. They were worried that they might miss Trevor and his new nanny but they needn't have fretted. When Alice Cleaver had disembarked, still clutching Trevor, she had initially been overwhelmed by the throng of reporters lobbying for her attention (and, for some reason, she told them her name was Jean). However, she quickly warmed up to the press, and they to her. The brothers found her surrounded by reporters, thoroughly enjoying her new position as the rescuer of the Allison heir.

Chapter 11
The City of Death

Even before the *Carpathia* reached New York, the White Star Line's Halifax agent, A. G. Jones and Company, was assigned the dreadful task of retrieving the *Titanic*'s victims. Jones commissioned a Halifax commercial cable ship, the *Mackay-Bennett*, to head up the recovery mission. John Snow and Company, the province's largest undertaker was hired to oversee the funeral arrangements. The job was too big for one company to handle, so an urgent call for help went out through the Maritime Funeral Directors Association. Soon, 40 embalmers — from Nova Scotia, New Brunswick, and Prince Edward Island — were on their way to help. Embalmer Annie F. O'Neil, of Saint John, New Brunswick, was assigned the gruelling task of embalming the women and children.

On Wednesday, April 17, Captain F. H. Lardner stood by as his ship was loaded with tons of ice, embalmers' tools, and more than a hundred coffins. His crew, all of whom had volunteered for the grisly task, were to receive double pay for the trip. Canon Kenneth O. Hind, from Halifax's All Saints Cathedral, came along to offer support to the sailors on their gruelling mission, and to provide a pastoral presence for the dead.

Once the *Mackay-Bennett* was underway, Captain Lardner radioed all other ships in the area, asking them to alert him if they saw any victims. By now most ships were giving the area a wide berth — some hoping to spare their passengers the trauma, others just trying to keep their ships away from the ice. But a few ships still ventured into the area. The liner *Bremen* reported having seen more than a hundred bodies floating in the water. Mrs. Johanna Stunke, one of its first-class passengers, later told reporters, "We saw the body of a woman dressed only in her nightdress and clasping a baby to her breast. Close by was the body of another woman with her arms tightly clasped around a shaggy dog."

The recovery ship didn't reach the spot where the *Titanic* had reportedly sunk until 8 p.m. on Saturday, April 20, almost eight days after the tragedy. They dropped anchor and waited for morning to start their grim task.

It was heavy, arduous work. As cable engineer Fredric A. Hamilton recorded in his diary, "The Ocean is strewn with a litter of woodwork, chairs, and bodies, and there are several growlers [icebergs] about. Hauling the soaked remains in saturated clothing over the side of the cutter is no light task. Fifty-one we have taken on board today [April 21] and still the sea seems strewn."

One body in particular, the fourth recovered, affected even the toughest sailors. It was the body of a small fair-haired boy, about two years old. "He came floating toward us with a little upturned face," John Snow, Jr., one of the embalmers, later told the *Halifax Herald*. His was the only body recovered without a life belt, and carried no identification. They dubbed him the "Unknown Child."

As each corpse was transferred from the pickup boat to the ship the job of identification began. A small square of canvas with a number stencilled on it was attached to each body. The contents of their pockets, including money and jewellery, were put into canvas bags bearing the same number. Then a full description of each victim was recorded, including height, weight, hair colour, age, and a list of any birthmarks, scars, or tattoos.

Body number 135 was pulled from the sea wearing a leather coat, blue suit, and grey silk muffler. In his pockets they found a set of keys, some letters and photos, a stock book, three pocket diaries, one Canadian Pacific Railway ticket book, two pocketbooks, a card case, a chain with insurance medals, a knife, and currency including £15 in gold, £35 in notes, $100 in Thomas Cook & Sons travellers' cheques, and $147.40 in cash. The man wore gold cuff links, a diamond solitaire ring, a gold stud, and a silver tie clip. Identification complete, Hud Allison's body was prepared for the long trip home.

Tagged as body number 292, Thomas McCaffry was still in his dress suit and brown overcoat when he was pulled from the water. His effects included a man's purse, a knife, a pocketbook, three studs, a gold chain, a locket, a watch, a pencil, sleeve links, pearl cuff links, and currency including £10 in notes, 40 lira, 19 shillings, and a few other coins. The monogram "T.C.Mc." embroidered on his underwear confirmed his identity.

Even in death, social protocol was observed. The first-class passengers were placed in coffins, the second-class passengers were sewn into canvas bags, and the third-class passengers were laid out on ice in the ship's hold. Many of the bodies retrieved were too broken to be embalmed or even identified, so it was decided to bury them at sea.

Fredric Hamilton noted in his diary:

At 8 p.m. [on April 21], the tolling of the bell summoned all hands to the forecastle where thirty bodies are ready to be committed to the deep, each carefully weighted and each carefully sewn up in canvas. It is a weird scene, this gathering. The crescent moon is shedding a faint light on us, as the ship lays wallowing in the great rollers. The funeral service is conducted by the Reverend Canon

Hind, for nearly an hour the words "For as much as it hath pleased the lord we therefore commit this body to the deep," are repeated, at each interval comes a splash, as the weighted body plunges into the sea, there to sink to a depth of about two miles [3.2 km]. Splash, splash, splash!

As the days wore on, the task of retrieving the bodies became overwhelming. At last, on April 22, the *Minia,* a cable ship owned by Anglo-American Telegraph, joined the search. Outfitted with tons of ice and 150 coffins it headed out to join the *Mackay-Bennett.* The first body they found was that of Charles Hays, identified by papers in his pocket and the name engraved on his watch.

From amidst the chairs, writing desks, cabin doors, and other debris, the *Mackay-Bennett* managed to retrieve 306 bodies, 116 of which were buried at sea. The remaining 190 were brought back to Halifax. In total, 328 bodies were retrieved from the water before gale winds swept the last of the *Titanic's* debris out into the Gulf Stream.

Back in Halifax, dubbed the "city of death" by newspapers, security was tight. Clergymen at local churches asked their congregants to stay away from the ship as it docked; most complied.

At George's Island, port physician W. D. Finn and various police officials boarded the *Mackay-Bennett.*

The Royal Canadian Naval Dockyard's north coaling

wharf number four was readied for the *Mackay-Bennett's* arrival. The dock's large concrete wall would help with crowd control and privacy. But before the *Mackay-Bennett* had even embarked on her mission, Jim Hickey, the news editor at the *Halifax Chronicle,* worked out a deal with Canon Hind. As the ship returned to port, Hickey waited out in the harbour on a hired tug. As arranged, Hind threw Hickey a container. Inside was a document listing the names of all the bodies the crew had managed to identify. Their names were published in the *Halifax Chronicle* even before the coroner's office had obtained the list.

As the ship eased into the dock, the medical examiner and deputy registrar boarded to issue death certificates and burial permits so the bodies could be removed from the ship. It took three hours to unload them all.

From the dock they were taken in horse-drawn hearses, as many as 10 at a time, up the long hill to the Mayflower Curling Rink on Agricola Street, which had been designated as the temporary morgue. Each body was photographed and, if necessary, embalmed. It was then placed in one of 67 temporary canvas rooms, each big enough to hold three bodies, to await identification by friends or family.

By now, Halifax's hotels were overflowing with people desperately hoping to find their loved ones. Cape Breton senator David McKeen was there, looking for Hugo Ross. Hudson Allison, whose body was one of the first released from the morgue, was shipped home to his brother in Montreal, then on to Chesterville, Ontario, where he was buried in the rural cemetery near Winchester. Bess's body was never recovered, nor was Loraine's.

Ross Kelly, vice-president of the Grand Trunk Railroad, had the awful task of claiming the body of Charles Hays, which travelled back to Montreal in its own private train car. His memorial service was conducted simultaneously in two churches, the American Presbyterian Church in Montreal and the Church of St. Edmund King and Martyr in London, England. At exactly 11:30 a.m. on May 8, five minutes of silence were observed across the entire Grand Trunk Railroad network. All railway activities were suspended as all employees stopped and bowed their heads in respect for their lost leader. Charles was buried in the Pine Hill section of Mount Royal cemetery overlooking the other tombstones. The inscription on his tombstone reads: "In Loving Memory of Charles Melville Hays. Born in Rock Island, Illinois, May 16, 1856. Died in the foundering of the S.S. *Titanic*, April 15, 1912. And so he died. And the example of his simple devoted consecrated life is our priceless heritage. We are different people and we are better people because this man lived and worked and loved and died."

Thomas McCaffry's body was also sent back to Montreal, where he was interned at the Notre Dame des Neiges cemetery. His grave is marked with a large granite tombstone purchased for him by his bank.

Makeshift memorial services sprung up all across the

county. On April 17, flags flew at half-mast in front of civic buildings in Winnipeg and Regina. The T. Eaton Company's Winnipeg department store was closed for a half a day to remember George Graham. Four days later a special Sunday mass was said for Quigg Baxter at Saint Patrick's Church in Montreal. Similar services were held for Harry Molson and Charles Hays's secretary, Vivian Payne, at Christ Church Anglican Cathedral. One hundred and twenty-three of Payne's associates later joined together to erect a memorial plaque in his name in the cathedral.

A large memorial stone was erected by the Molson family in memory of Harry at Montreal's Mount Royal Cemetery, the epitaph captured in brass quoting Psalm 77, verse 19: "Thy way is in the sea, and Thy path in the great waters, and Thy footsteps are not known."

To mark the loss of Mark and Charles Fortune, neither of whose bodies were ever recovered, a new set of chimes was installed in Winnipeg's Knox United Church. A memorial plaque to Winnipeg's six local *Titanic* victims was also installed at city hall. It reads: "Erected by the People of Winnipeg in memory of Their Fellow Citizens Mark Fortune; John Hugo Ross; Thompson Beattie; Charles A. Fortune; George E. Graham; and J. J. Borebank Who with 1484 others lost their lives when the Steamship *Titanic* Founded in mid-Atlantic April 15, 1912. They died that women and children might live." The plaque still hangs in the passageway that links the old administration building to the new city council chambers. Each man also had a street in Winnipeg named after him.

Not every body claim went without a snag. When Catherine Harbeck came from Toledo, Ohio, to claim the body of her husband, cinematographer William Harbeck, officials labelled her an impostor. It seems the White Star Line's records showed that a "Mrs. Harbeck" had been travelling on the *Titanic* with William and had drowned. It was never determined whether the so-named woman travelling with William was a relative, a mistress, or another wife, but there was a definite connection. William was pulled from the ocean clutching the other woman's purse, his wedding ring inside it. The real Mrs. Harbeck escorted William's body back to Toledo, where he was hastily buried in an unmarked grave.

One of the Halifax embalmers, Frank Newell, also got the shock of his life when he encountered the body of his uncle, Arthur W. Newell, president of the Boston Fourth National Bank. Newell had been on the *Titanic* with his two daughters. Luckily, both girls survived.

Bodies not claimed or identified, or whose families couldn't afford to ship them home, were buried in one of Halifax's three cemeteries: the non-secular Fairview Cemetery, the Jewish Baron de Hirsch Cemetery, or the Catholic Mount Olivet Cemetery At times it took some guesswork to determine who should be buried where. Using the ship's records, information from relatives, and sometimes just the spelling of the victim's name, clerks did their best to sort it all out. At one point, however, Rabbi Jacob Walter chose to take matters into his own hands. He declared that 10 bodies waiting for burial at the Fairmont Cemetery were actually Jewish, and he sent people to retrieve them and bring them to the Baron de Hirsh Cemetery. However, the authorities flatly refused to alter the burial certificates. They produced records showing that four of the dead were Catholic and that the families of the other six had requested burial at the Fairmont. The standoff lasted two days before the rabbi finally gave in and returned the bodies to the Fairmont.

In the end, Rabbi Walter did end up with one extra body, that of Michel Navratill, a second-class passenger who had been travelling to the United States from France under the name of Hoofman. A devoted Catholic, Navratill was travelling with his two sons — Edmond, aged two, and Michel, aged three — whom he had recently kidnapped from his estranged wife. The boys, fortunately, survived the sinking. But their father did not. Because of the name under which he travelled, Hoofman, the clerks believed Navratill to be Jewish. He was buried in the Baron de Hirsh Cemetery before the situation came to light. The boys were eventually reunited with their mother.

It has often been said that truth is stranger than fiction. Nowhere was this demonstrated more vividly than with the story of the "unknown child." On Saturday, May 4, everything in Halifax stopped for the little boy's funeral. The White Star Line had been swamped with offers to sponsor his funeral, but they decided to give that honour to the crew of the *Mackay-Bennett.* St. George's Anglican Church was filled to capacity with people and flowers. Captain Lardner and all 75 crew members were in attendance. The small white coffin, heaped with flowers, was carried from the church on the shoulders of six crew members; it travelled to the Fairview Cemetery in a horse-drawn hearse. With hundreds looking on, the unknown child was laid to rest on the western edge of the cemetery on a hill overlooking Fairview Cove. On his headstone were carved the words, "Erected to the Memory of an Unknown Child Whose Remains Were Recovered after the Disaster to the *Titanic,* April 15, 1912."

The little boy was buried in a plot adjacent to the grave of third-class passenger Alma Paulson. Paulson was a 29-year-old Swedish woman who, along with her four children, had perished on the *Titanic.* In 2001 scientists from Ontario's Lakehead University, using DNA testing, established that the Unknown Child was actually Eino Viljami, Paulson's 13-month-old son.

Of the 328 bodies recovered, 59 were eventually claimed by relatives and taken elsewhere for burial. One hundred and fifty bodies were buried in one of Halifax's three cemeteries; to date (2006), 128 of those have still not been identified.

Chapter 12
The Years After

After reaching New York, Alice Cleaver and the Allisons' two other surviving servants, Sarah Daniels and Mildred Brown, accompanied Trevor Allison and his uncles on the train back to Montreal. Little Trevor was immediately handed over to his Aunt Lillian and Uncle George. Cleaver and the other servants were put up at the Windsor hotel in Montreal.

At the outset, Cleaver was heralded a heroine by the press. However, it didn't take long for the Allison family to start questioning her story and they were soon blaming her for the loss of Hud, Bess, and Loraine. Newspapers labelled her rush to the lifeboat as selfish act of cowardice.

Then another sensational story broke. It seemed that, in 1909, Miss Alice Cleaver had been charged with murder in

England. The record showed that she had, with forethought, thrown her newborn son from a train. At the time of her trial Miss Cleaver had strongly denied any wrongdoing, passionately maintaining she had given up the child for adoption to a Mrs. Gray in Tottenham. The court was not convinced. Cleaver was convicted of murder and shipped off to prison. Eventually, the story went, she was pardoned by a kindly judge who attributed her act to depression resulting from having given birth out of wedlock and to being deserted by the child's father.

The newspapers had a field day. Alice adamantly denied the story, but the damage was done. No longer the sweetheart rescuer, she quickly disappeared from the public eye, leaving a trail of speculation behind her. However, Cleaver's denials were probably true. Trevor's new nursemaid was very likely exactly what she professed herself to be — Alice Catherine Cleaver, an innocent, inexperienced young woman just looking for a decent job and a better life. She maintained that she'd done nothing wrong, claiming she had done her best to dress the hysterical Bess and the children. But when she saw she would never get Bess to act rationally, it had become her job to save Trevor, which she did.

And the horrible story about killing her own baby? Alice claimed, of course, that it was completely false. And again, she was probably telling the truth. Indeed, court records showed that a lady named Alice Mary Cleaver had been convicted of throwing her baby off a train, but there seemed to be some question as to whether she was ever released. Most likely she died in prison.

Under a dark cloud of suspicion, Alice Cleaver returned to England. In time, she married Edward James Williams, a surgical appliance manufacturer, and they had two daughters. Cleaver died of a stroke in 1984 at the age of 96. Trevor Allison, the baby she had saved, predeceased her by 55 years. He died of food poisoning in Maine on August 7, 1929, just three months after his 18th birthday. He was buried at the Maple Ridge Cemetery in Chesterville, alongside his father.

And what about the horses Hud had purchased in Scotland? They were much luckier than their master. They crossed the ocean on a tramp steamer, landing safe and sound, much to the surprise of his brothers when they showed up at the farm nearly a month after Hud's funeral.

The Fortune women checked into the suite at the Belmont Hotel that Mark had reserved for them. Mrs. Fortune's brother-in-law, H. C. Hutton, who was also a Winnipeg real estate broker, travelled to New York to retrieve them. He fielded reporters' questions, saying the women were much too grief-stricken to make any statements, and then escorted them back to Winnipeg.

Ethel Fortune kept her promise and married Crawford Gordon in 1913. Seven years later the Gordons moved to Jamaica. Crawford was then appointed manager of the U.K. Bank of Commerce, so they emigrated to England. Their son, Crawford Gordon II, became head of the Canadian aircraft manufacturing plant A. V. Roe, which, in the 1950s, produced the Avro Arrow, the world's most advanced and shortest-lived military aircraft. Ethel died in Toronto on March 22, 1961. She is buried in Toronto's Mount Pleasant Cemetery.

On June 8, 1912, Alice Fortune married Charles Holden Allen, a lawyer originally from New Brunswick. The couple had one daughter, Mary McDougald Norris (née Allen). Together they purchased a vacation home in Chester, Nova Scotia, where they would later retire. Alice died on April 7, 1961. She was laid to rest in the Bayview Anglican cemetery in Chester, beside her husband Charles who had died six years earlier.

Alice's gentleman friend, William Sloper, also survived the sinking. It was rumoured that he was the man who had entered a lifeboat dressed in women's clothing, but that was far from the truth. In fact, he left the ship in lifeboat 7, one of the lifeboats loaded by Officer Murdock. It was Murdock who, when no more women were available, had allowed men into his boats. Sloper made his way home to Connecticut. He died in 1955.

The shock of the sinking did not cause Mabel Fortune to forget her first love. Back home in Canada, in 1913, she and musician Harrison Driscoll were married. They had one son, Robert, but, as her parents had predicted, it was a short-lived arrangement. Mabel left Driscoll, enrolled Robert in a boarding school, and moved in with Charlotte Armstrong, a woman she had met in Ottawa. Mabel died in Victoria, British

Columbia on February 19, 1968, at the age of 79. She is buried in the Royal Oak Burial Park, in Victoria.

Not long after the sinking, Mary Fortune sold the house on Wellington Crescent. It still stands on the same spot but, unfortunately, is just outside of the jurisdiction of the Crescentwood Homeowners' Association, a group set up to protect historic Winnipeg mansions. It was divided into three suites, with its original interior destroyed.

Mary never remarried. She died in Toronto on March 8, 1929, almost 17 years after the sinking, when she was 76. Mary is memorialized on the wall of the indoor cenotaph at Mount Pleasant Cemetery.

The morning after the survivors reached New York, Clara Hays was reported to be in a "state of collapse." She was hurried off to New York's Grand Central Station where she boarded a special train that took home her to Montreal. She then headed to Ottawa for the birth of her grandson. He came into the world without complications on April 23, and was christened Thornton Davidson in honour of his uncle.

The official opening of the Château Laurier Hotel in Ottawa was postponed then cancelled. Six weeks later, quietly and with no official opening ceremony, but with hundreds of onlookers, the hotel opened its doors for business. Prime Minister Sir Wilfrid Laurier signed the register as its first guest.

Laurier had described Charles as "the greatest railroad genius in Canada" and a "valued acquisition to Canada," and many believed it was his death that signalled the end of the Grand Trunk Railway. As early as 1914, in the hope of staying afloat, the Grand Trunk and the Canadian Pacific Railway formed a subsidiary company, the Grand Trunk Pacific Railway, but the partnership suffered heavy financial losses. The Grand Truck was forced to declare bankruptcy in 1919. Four years later the federal government placed the Grand Trunk's assets under the control of Canadian National Railways. A grand era in Canadian railroad history had ended.

After the sinking, Clara spent much of her time at their summer home on Cushing Island, in Casco Bay, Maine. She died on February 1, 1955. She was 96. She is buried in the Mount Royal cemetery, in Montreal, next to Charles.

The railcar from Charles's funeral train is still on display at the Canadian Railway Museum near Delson, Quebec. Prince Rupert, British Columbia, a town founded for the railways, also memorialized Charles. A mountain and a creek are named after him. And *Charlie's,* a local restaurant, proudly displays the local newspaper's front page announcing Hays's death on the *Titanic.* There is also a prominent statue of Charles in the centre of Prince Rupert, right next to the city hall. In 1992, Charles Hays Secondary School was opened in his honour.

The death by drowning of Thornton Davidson, Orian's husband, was a further blow to his already shattered family. Five years earlier, Thornton's brother, Shirley, and his fiancée,

Eileen Hingston, had drowned in Lake St. Louis in what was reportedly a boating accident. Many believed that, in fact, the young couple had committed suicide after Thornton's father, Quebec Supreme Court Judge Charles Peers Davidson, refused to give them his blessing — Hingston was a Roman Catholic and the Davidsons were Protestant.

Following the disaster, Hélène Baxter returned to Montreal, but she never quite recovered from the loss of her son, Quigg. She died in her apartment on June 19, 1923. She is buried with her husband, Jim, in the Baxter family plot in the Notre Dame de Neiges cemetery.

Upon returning home Zette contracted a mild case of polio, and she was fitted with a leg brace to help her walk. Fredrick started drinking heavily and lost his hospital privileges, forcing the couple to relocate to Sherbrooke, Quebec. After Hélène's death Zette was finally free to leave Fredrick. She moved back to Montreal and married stockbroker Edgar Cole Richardson. In the early 1930s the couple moved to Redland, California. Zette died on the last day of December in 1954, at the age of 70. She willed her family's heirlooms to her Canadian relatives, but no one stepped forward to pay to have them shipped back to Montreal. What happened to them is just another of the *Titanic*'s lingering mysteries.

After a brief stay in Montreal, Berthe headed back to Brussels. She later travelled to Paris to resume her career and, in 1913, graced the cover of *Music-Hall Illustrée,* under the name Bella Vielly. Clearly still travelling in the same circles, she formed a long-time liaison with Monsieur Henri Cot, a Brussels steel manufacturer. Together they returned to Brussels in 1924.

Because of her reputation for tall tales, Berthe's family always questioned her story of being on the *Titanic* and her engagement to a rich, young French Canadian. After her death in October of 1962, they found, among her possessions, a cache of memorabilia including photos of Quigg and of the Baxter house in Montreal, and various other pieces of evidence proving that she had, indeed, been on the stricken ship. Berthe was buried at Ste-Agathe's Cemetery, in Berchem Sainte-Agathe, Belgium.

After disembarking from the *Carpathia* Major Arthur Peuchen checked into New York's Waldorf Hotel. Five days later he testified in front of the United States Senate Hearing into the sinking of the *Titanic,* recalling the events of that fateful night. When he was done he headed back to his commission in Toronto, and by the next spring was promoted to Lieutenant-Colonel. At the start of World War I he left the Standard Chemical Company to command the Home Battalion of the Queen's Own Rifles. He was awarded the Officer's Long Service Decoration.

Like many of the men who survived the sinking, Peuchen was haunted all his life by the fact that he had lived when so many others, especially women and children, had died. Many branded him a coward for leaving the ship before the women, saying he had used the fact that he was a yachtsman to hide his cowardice and save himself. It was even said that people had crossed the street so as not to have to walk by him.

In 1920 Peuchen and the McLaren Lumber Company embarked on a project to build a dam on the Oldman River, in southwestern Alberta. The project was plagued with cost overruns and winter ice floe delays, and then the market fell out of the lumber business. Consequently the project was abandoned and the dam was not built until 1992.

By the mid-1920s, as a result of some bad investments, Peuchen was said to be practically broke. It was even rumoured that he spent his last four years living in the company's dormitory in Hinton, Alberta. He returned to Toronto in 1929, where he passed away on December 7 of that same year. He was 71. Major Peuchen is buried in Mount Pleasant Cemetery in Toronto.

In 1987 a salvage team recovered Peuchen's wallet from the debris surrounding the wreckage. In it they found his calling card, a traveller's cheque, and some streetcar tickets.

Quartermaster Hichen denied all allegations that he had ever acted improperly. However, his temper would again get the better of him. One night, in a drunken stupor, he pulled a gun and shot a friend whom he believed had wronged him over the purchase of a sailboat. Fortunately the bullet only grazed his target. He then turned the gun on himself, with similar dismal results. Hichen spent four years in prison for the shooting. He died in September of 1940, three years after being released.

A full month after the accident, the White Star ship *Oceanic* stumbled across a small open lifeboat floating alone in the Atlantic, some 300 kilometres southeast of where the *Titanic* had sunk. The sideless boat turned out to be collapsible A. The crew was amazed to discover that it still contained the bodies of the three passengers left behind by Officer Lowe. The bodies had been bleached by the sun and the salt, and were in an advanced state of decomposition. The *Oceanic* immediately dispatched a lifeboat, with an officer and a medical official to investigate. One of the bodies in the boat was that of Thomas Beattie. Still neatly dressed in his evening clothes, he was identified by his watch, the papers in his overcoat, and the labels on his clothing, which showed his name and that of the dealer.

After identification, each of the bodies was sewn into a canvas sack with a heavy metal rod at its feet, draped in the Union Jack, and, after a short ceremony, returned to the sea. In another of truth's strange double coincidences, the three were buried at sea on May 15, the birthday of Thomas Beattie's mother, Janet — at almost exactly the same spot in the Atlantic where, some 82 years earlier, she had been born on the ocean liner *Justinian*.

The discovery of the three men in collapsible A threw the newspapers into another wild round of frenzied speculation. They wondered, had the three men been merely unconscious that night, and later died of exposure or starvation? One story in the *St. Paul News* said the men had been found with pieces of cork and wood in their mouths, and that teeth marks could be seen on the boat, suggesting that they'd been trying to eat the boat to survive. No concrete evidence was ever found that the men were alive when Lowe left them.

In the fall of 1940 another bizarre story hit the news, this time in the *Philadelphia Inquirer.* The piece, under the headline "Alien Told She Escaped From the *Titanic,"* told the story of Mrs. Laurence Kramer, a British citizen, who was attempting to convince the U.S. Alien Registration Board in Detroit, Michigan (the department in charge of foreigners entering the United States) that she was actually Loraine Allison.

She alleged that she had, for the last 28 years, believed herself to be the daughter of English parents. When she requested her birth certificate so she could live in Michigan with her American husband, her father wrote her back saying he didn't have one. The letter went on to say that she wasn't really his daughter. He said that while he and his wife waited on the deck of the *Titanic* for a place in a lifeboat, a stranger had thrust her into his arms. The man had identified himself as H. J. Allison from Pennsylvania, and the girl as his daughter, Loraine. He begged the man who was waiting in line to take her, as he wanted to make sure she got off the ship safely. But he was intent on returning to get his wife and their small son.

Lorraine Allison Kramer now alleged that Hud and Bess were her real parents and Trevor was her biological brother, but her story was full of holes. First, the girls spelled their names differently — Kramer as "Lorraine" and the daughter of Hud and Bess as "Loraine." And then there was the fact that the real Loraine Allison was born in Ontario, not Pennsylvania.

Some speculated that Kramer's ruse was the work of Alice Cleaver. After all she knew practically everything about the Allisons. But then, so did almost anyone who could read. And those who knew Mrs. Alice Williams (née Cleaver) in England, dismissed the story as malicious gossip, saying she was a delightful old lady who rarely spoke of the Allisons or of her time on the *Titanic*. In any event, with her story apparently unravelling Lorraine Kramer disappeared, along with any claim she might have made against the Allison estate. If Lorraine Kramer was one of the Allison family, she was, it seemed, luckier not to have shared their fortunes.

Epilogue
The Legend
Lives On

She was the largest craft afloat and the greatest of the works of men. In her construction and mainte-nance were involved every science, profession, and trade known to civilization ...

From the bridge, engine-room, and a dozen places on her deck the ninety-two doors of nineteen water-tight compartments could be closed in half a minute by turning a lever ...

With nine compartments flooded the ship would still float, and so no known accident of the sea could possibly fill this many, the steamship Titan *was considered practically unsinkable.*

Built of steel throughout, and for passenger traffic only ... She was eight hundred feet long, of seventy thousand tons displacement, seventy-five thousand horse-power, and on her trial trip had steamed at a rate of twenty-five knots an hour over the bottom, in the face of unconsidered winds, tides, and currents. In short, she was a floating city — containing within her steel walls all that tends to minimize the dangers and discomforts of the Atlantic voyage — all that makes life enjoyable.

Unsinkable — indestructible, she carried as few boats as would satisfy the laws. These, twenty-four in number, were securely covered and lashed down to their chocks on the upper deck ...

– Excerpt from U.S. futurist Morgan Robertson's 1898 book *Futility*

Did Morgan Robertson prophesy the sinking of the *Titanic* 14 years before it happened, in his book *Futility*? Or was he, like Charles Hays, just stating the obvious conclusion — that it was only a matter of time?

What is it about the gigantic ship that grips our imagination so tightly? The *Titanic* is not the biggest ship ever made. No sooner had she slipped beneath the waves, than Germany launched the *Imperator,* the world's first liner in excess of 50,000 tons. Even the *Titanic's* sister vessel, the *Britannic,* was larger, wider, and boasted more gross tonnage than the infamous ship. And she was not the biggest ship to sink; to date (2006), the *Britannic* holds that record. She isn't even the ship that sank the most rapidly. The *Empress of Ireland,* which went down in the fog-shrouded St. Lawrence River in

1914, sank in a mere 14 minutes. And she took with her 1,012 souls — eight more than were lost on the *Titanic.*

However, the *Titanic* was a symbol of a better time, a time of opulence and security. Before she sank, the world had enjoyed nearly a hundred years of peace (a peace that would soon be shattered by the outbreak of World War I) and a stretch of industrial progress that had moved along at an astonishing rate. People were prepared to believe that anything was possible, even an unsinkable ship.

So when the *Titanic* settled to the bottom of the ocean that day in April, she took with her more than her passengers and crew. She also took our innocence. Nothing would ever be unsinkable again.

Even now, as the gigantic ship rots slowly on the ocean floor, we cannot seem to shake her legacy. Her crow's nest, from where lookout Frederick Fleet first glimpsed the fatal iceberg, has already vanished. The forward mast has crumpled, leaving behind a gaping hole in her deck. Roy Cullimore, a microbiologist with Droycon Bioconcepts in Regina, Saskatchewan, has taken into account the effect of the marine environment on the great ship. If his calculations are correct, rust, salt, and sea creatures will have eaten away the *Titanic's* entire external structure by 2028.

Even after she has completely turned to dust, the *Titanic* will still fascinate future generations who, like us, long for that quieter, more elegant time. A time when the giants of the sea ruled the world and anything was possible.

Appendix
Passengers Travelling to Canada

(Asterisks denote those who did not survive the sinking of the *Titanic*.)

FIRST CLASS

*Allison, Hudson Joshua Creighton (nickname Hud), age 30. Land developer, businessman, Winnipeg. Born December 9, 1881. (Married Bess Daniels December 9, 1907.)

*Allison, Bess Waldo (née Daniels), age 25. Born November 14, 1886.

*Allison, Helen Loraine, age 2. Born June 5, 1909.

Allison, Hudson Trevor, age 11 months. Born May 7, 1911. Lifeboat 11. Died, food poisoning, August 7, 1929.

Baxter, Hélène Chaput, age 50. Widow. Born Joliette, Quebec, March 29, 1862. Lifeboat 6. Died Montreal, June 19, 1923.

*Baxter, Quigg Edmond, age 24. Born Montreal, July 13, 1887.

*Beattie, Thomson, age 36. Landowner, businessman, Winnipeg. Born Fergus, Ontario, November 25, 1873.

*Borebank, John James, age 42. Real estate broker, Toronto. Born Derbyshire, England, 1870.

Cherry, Gladys, age 30. Travelling to BC with her cousin the Countess of Rothes. Born August 27, 1881. Lifeboat 8. Died May 4, 1965.

Chevré, Paul Romain, age 45. Sculptor who divided his time equally between France and Canada. Born Brussels, July 5, 1866. Lifeboat 9. Died February 20, 1914.

Cleaver, Alice Catherine, age 22. Nursemaid to Trevor Allison. Born July 5, 1889. Lifeboat 11. Died November 1, 1984.

*Colley, Edward Pomeroy, age 37. Mining broker, Victoria. Born Kildare, Ireland, April 15, 1875.

Daniel, Sarah, age 33. Personal maid to Bess Allison. Lifeboat 8.

*Davidson, Thornton, age 31. Banker, Montreal. Born May 17, 1880. Married Orian Hays, November 3, 1906.

Davidson, Orian (née Hays), age 27. Born November 18, 1884. Lifeboat 3. Died May 3, 1979.

Dick, Albert Adrian, age 31. Real estate investor, Alberta. Born Winnipeg, July 29, 1880. (Married Vera Gillespie May 31, 1911.) Lifeboat 3. Died September 8, 1970.

Dick, Vera (née Gillespie), age 17. Born June 12, 1894, Died Banff, Alberta, October 7, 1973.

Douglas, Mary Suzette Hélène (née Baxter), age 27. Born April 4, 1885. Died December 31, 1954.

*Fortune, Mark, age 64. Businessman, Winnipeg. Born Carluke, Ontario, November 2, 1847. (Married Mary McDougald.)

Fortune, Mary (née McDougald), age 60. Born May 12, 1851. Lifeboat 10. Died Toronto March 8, 1929.

Fortune, Ethel Flora, age 28. Born September 22, 1883. Lifeboat 10. (Married Crawford Gordon 1913.) Died in Toronto, March 22, 1961.

Fortune, Alice Elizabeth, age 24. Born May 10, 1887. Lifeboat 10. (Married Charles Allen August 28, 1880.) Died April 8, 1961.

Fortune, Mabel Helen, age 23. Born November 3, 1888. Lifeboat 10. (Married Harrison Driscoll 1913.) Died February 19, 1968.

*Fortune, Charles Alexander, age 19. Born October 13, 1892.

*Graham, George, age 38. Sales manager, the T. Eaton Company. Born St. Mary's, Ontario, June 11, 1873.

Appendix

*Hays, Charles Melville, age 55.
President, Grand Trunk Railway.
Born May 16, 1856. (Married
Clara Gregg in St. Louis, Missouri,
October 13, 1881.)

Hays, Clara Jennings (née Gregg),
age 52. Born October 13, 1859.
Lifeboat 3. Died, Montreal,
February 1, 1955.

Lesneur (or possibly Lesueur),
Gustave, age 35. Originally from
Ottawa, manservant to Mr. Thomas
Cardeza of Philadelphia. Lifeboat 3.
(No death date recorded.)

Maioni (or possibly Maloni),
Ruberta Elizabeth Mary, age 19.
Personal maid to the Countess of
Rothes. Born 1892. Lifeboat 8. Died
January 17, 1963.

Mayné, Berthe Antonine (registered
under the name Mrs. de Villiers),
age 24. Cabaret singer. Born Lxelles,
Belgium, July 21, 1887. Lifeboat 6.
Died October 11, 1962.

*McCaffry (or possibly McCaffrey),
Thomas Francis, age 46. Banker,
Vancouver. Born Three Rivers,
Quebec, February 5, 1866.

*Molson, Harry Markland, age 55.
Born Montreal, August 9, 1856.

*Partner, Austen, age 40.
Stockbroker. Travelling to Toronto
and Winnipeg on business. Born
November 30, 1871.

*Payne, Vivian Ponsonby, age 22.
Charles Hays's personal secretary.
Born in 1889.

Perreault, Anne, age 33. Mrs. Clara
Hays's personal maid. Born Saint-
Majorique, Quebec, July 29, 1878.
Lifeboat 3. Died November 18, 1968.
(Anne's surname is spelled "Perrault"
on her death certificate and
"Perreault" on her marriage certifi-
cate. The latter is probably correct.)

Peuchen, Major Arthur Godfrey,
age 52. President, Standard
Chemical Company. Born
Montreal, April 19, 1859. Lifeboat
6. Died Toronto, December 7, 1929.

*Ross, John Hugo, age 36. Real
estate broker, Winnipeg. Born
November 24, 1875. Collapsible A.

Rothes, Countess of (née Edwards,
Lucy Noël Martha), age 33.
Travelling to British Columbia
to be with her husband. Born
December 25, 1878. (Married
Norman Evelyn Leslie the 19th Earl
of Rothes, April 19, 1900.) Lifeboat
8. Died September 12, 1956.

*Wright, George, age 62. Publisher of the *Wrights World Business Directories*. Born Tufts Cove, Nova Scotia, October 26, 1849.

SECOND CLASS

Brown, Amelia Marry (Mildred), age 18. Cook to the Allison family. Born August 18, 1893. Lifeboat 11. Died June 30, 1976.

Christy, Alice Frances, age 45. Travelling to Montreal. Lifeboat 12. Died July 7, 1939.

Christy, Rachel Julie Cohen, age 25. Travelling to Montreal. Lifeboat 12. Died October 30, 1931.

*Davies, Charles Henry, age 21. Travelling from England to Eden, Manitoba. Born 1890.

*Deacon, Percy William, age 17. Travelling from England to Eden, Manitoba. Born 1892.

*Dibden, William, age 18. Travelling from England to Eden, Manitoba. Born October 29, 1893.

*Fynney, Joseph, age 35. Rubber merchant travelling from England to Montreal. Born 1876. *Minia*, body 322.

*Gaskell, Alfred, age 16. Apprentice barrel-maker travelling from England to Montreal. Born 1896.

*Gillespie, William Henry, age 34. Clerk travelling from Ireland to Vancouver.

*Harbeck, William, H. age 44, Cinematographer. U.S. citizen travelling to Montreal. Born 1863. *Mackay-Bennett*, body 35.

*Hart, Benjamin, age 47. Builder travelling from England to Winnipeg. Born December 25, 1864.

Hart, Esther, age 48. Born May 13, 1865. Lifeboat 14. Died September 7, 1928.

Hart, Eva, age 7. Born January 31, 1905. Lifeboat 14. Died February 14, 1996.

*Hickman, Leonard Mark, age 24. Farmhand, Eden, Manitoba. Born September 18, 1887.

*Hickman, Lewis, age 30. Emigrating from England to The Pas, Manitoba. Born August 29, 1881. *Mackay-Bennett*, body 256.

Appendix

*Hickman, Stanley George, age 20. Emigrating from England to The Pas, Manitoba.

*Hood Ambrose, Jr., age 22. Travelling from England with Charles Davies. Born 1890.

*Jacobsohn, Sidney Samuel, age 40. Travelling from England to Montreal.

Jacobsohn, Amy Frances Christy (née Cohen), age 24. Travelling from England to Montreal. Died July 9, 1947.

*Kirkland, Rev. Charles Leonard (Levy), age 57. Minister, visiting Tuxford, Saskatchewan.

*Lévy, René Jacques, age 36. Chemist. Born Paris, 1875, emigrated to Montreal in 1910.

*Mallet, Albert, age 31. Merchant, Montreal. Born in France.

Mallet, André, age 1. Born Montreal, June 11, 1910. Lifeboat 10. Died September 1973.

Mallet, Antoinette, age 24. Born France, December 16, 1887. Lifeboat 10. Died October 22, 1974.

*Maybery, Frank, age 36. Real estate broker. Born November 30, 1875.

*McCrie, Matthew, James, age 30. Oil rig worker, Sarnia, Ontario.

*Norman, Robert Douglas, age 28. Born 1884. Electronic engineer, emigrating from Scotland to Vancouver. Born 1884. *Mackay-Bennett*, body 287.

*Pain, Dr. Alfred, age 23. Physician, Hamilton, Ontario. Born August 24, 1888.

*Richard, Emile Phillippe, age 23. Visiting Montreal from France.

*Sjostedt, Ernst Adolf, age 59. Mountain engineer, Sault Ste. Marie, Ontario. Born Sweden, September 9, 1852.

Slayter, Hilda, Mary, age 30. Born April 5, 1882. Halifax. Lifeboat 13. Died April 12, 1965.

*Swane, George, age 26. Chauffeur for Hud Allison. Born England, 1885. *Mackay-Bennett*, body 294.

*Weisz, Leopold. Artist. Emigrating from England to Montreal. *Mackay-Bennett*, body 293.

Weisz, Mathilde Françoise (née Pëde), age 37. Emigrating from England to Montreal with husband Leopold. Born May 1874. Lifeboat 10. Died October 13, 1953.

*Yvois (or possibly Yrois), Henriette, age 24. Travelling from France to Montreal.

THIRD CLASS

*Andersson, Anders Johan, age 39. Emigrating from Sweden to Winnipeg. Born January 1873. (Married to Alfrida.)

*Andersson, Alfrida Konstantia (née Brogren), age 39. Emigrating from Sweden to Winnipeg. Born December 25, 1872.

*Andersson, Ebba Iris Alfrida, age 6. Born November 14, 1905.

*Andersson, Ellis Anna Maria, age 2. Born January 19, 1910.

*Andersson, Ingeborg Constancia, age 9. Born April 16, 1902.

*Andersson, Sigrid Elizabeth, age 11. Born April 16, 1900.

*Andersson, Siyard Harald Elias, age 4. Born July, 21, 1908.

Assaf, Mariana (née Khalil), age 45. Born 1867. Collapsible C.

*Assaf, Gerios Thamah, age 21. Farmhand travelling from Lebanon to Ottawa.

*Attala, Sleiman, age 27. Journalist, Ottawa.

*Barbara, Catherine David, age 45. Housekeeper, emigrating from Lebanon to Ottawa.

*Barbara, Saiide, age 18. Housekeeper, emigrating from Lebanon to Ottawa.

*Boulos (or possibly Boulous), Sultan (or possibly Sultani), age 40. Emigrating from Lebanon to Kent, Ontario.

*Boulos, Akar, age 9. Emigrating from Lebanon to Kent, Ontario.

*Boulos, Hanna, 18. General labourer, travelling from Lebanon to Ottawa.

*Boulos, Nourclain, age 7. Emigrating from Lebanon to Kent, Ontario.

*Braund, Lewis Richard, age 29. Farmhand, emigrating

from England to Qu'Appelle Valley, Saskatchewan. Born 1883.

Braund, Owen Harris, age 22. Ironmonger, emigrating from England to Qu'Appelle Valley, Saskatchewan. Born 1889.

*Caram, Joseph, age 28. Merchant, travelling from Lebanon to Ottawa.

*Caram, Maria, age 18. Housekeeper, travelling from Lebanon to Ottawa.

*Colbert, Patrick, age 25. Travelling from Ireland to Sherbrooke, Quebec. Born November 5, 1887.

*Danbom, Ernst Gilbert, age 34. Farmer, emigrant recruiter for the U.S., travelling to Winnipeg to visit relatives. Born October 26, 1877. *Mackay-Bennett,* body 197.

*Danbom, Anna Sigrid Maria (née Brogren), age 28. U.S. citizen travelling to Winnipeg for a visit. Born March 10, 1884.

*Danbom, Gilbert Sigvard, age 4 months. Born November 16, 1911.

*Dennis, William, age 26. Farmer, emigrating from England to Saskatoon,

Saskatchewan. Born 1886.

*Dennis, Samuel, age 26. farmer, emigrating from England to Saskatoon, Saskatchewan. Born June 1899.

*Dika, Mirko, age 17. Travelling from Croatia to Vancouver.

*Elias, Joseph, Travelling from Lebanon to Ottawa with sons Joseph Jr. and Tannous.

*Elias, Joseph Jr., late teens. General labourer, travelling from Lebanon to Ottawa.

*Elias, Tannous, late teens to early 20s. General labourer, travelling from Lebanon to Ottawa.

Garfirth, John, 21. Shoemaker, travelling from Ireland to Kitchener.

*Hanna, Mansour, 35. Travelling from Lebanon to Ottawa. *Mackay-Bennett,* body 188.

*Johansion, Jakob Alfred, age 35. General labourer, travelling from Finland to Vancouver. Born June 11, 1877. *Mackay-Bennett,* body 143.

*Kallio, Nikolai Erland, age 17(?).
General labourer, travelling
from Finland to Sudbury. Born
December 18, 1894.

Krekorian, Neshan, age 25. General
labourer, travelling from Turkey
to Brantford, Ontario. Born
May 12, 1886. Lifeboat 10. Died
May 21, 1978.

*Lovell, John Hall (Henry),
age 20. Emigrating from England
to Canada. Born 1892 (?).

*Livshin, David Abraham, age 25.
Watchmaker, emigrating from
England to Montreal.

*Mäenpää, Matti Alexanteri,
age 23. Emigrating from Finland
to Sudbury. Born October 7, 1889.

*Mardirosian, Sarkis, age 25. Farm
labourer, travelling from Turkey to
Brantford.

*Morrow, Thomas Rowan,
age 30. General labourer,
Gleichen, Alberta. Born Ireland,
April 26, 1881.

*Nirva, Isakki Antion Äijö, age 41.
General labourer, emigrating
from Finland to Sudbury. Born
December 24, 1870.

*Nofal (or possibly Novel),
Mansouer, age 20. Journalist,
travelling from Lebanon to Ottawa.
Mackay-Bennett, body 181.

*Olsen, Ole Martin, age 27.
Travelling from Norway to
Broderick, Ontario. Born 1885.

*O'Sullivan, Bridget, age 21.
Emigrating from Ireland to
Montreal. Born May 18, 1890.

*Patchett, George, age 19.
Emigrating from England to
Kitchener. Born 1893.

*Perkin, John Henry, age 22.
Farmer, emigrating from England
to Saskatoon, Saskatchewan.
Born 1889.

Reynolds, Harold J., age 21. Baker,
emigrating from England to
Toronto. Born 1891. *Montmagny,*
body 327.

*Rintamäki, Matti, age 35. General
labourer, emigrating from Finland
to Sudbury. Born February 4, 1877.

*Sirayanian, Orsen, age 22.
Emigrating from Turkey to
Brantford, Ontario.

Appendix

Vartunian, David, age 22. General labourer, emigrating from Turkey to Brantford. Born April 1890. Lifeboat 13. Died August 3, 1966.

*Wiklund, Karl Johan, mid to late 20s. General labourer, emigrating from Finland to Montreal.

*Wiklund, Jacob Alfred, age 18(?). General labourer, emigrating from Finland to Montreal. *Minia,* body 314.

*Wiseman, Phillippe, age 54. Merchant, travelling from England to Quebec City.

*Zarkarian, Mapriededer, age 22. Emigrating from Turkey to Brantford. *Mackay-Bennett,* body 304.

*Zarkarian, Ortin, age 27. General labourer, emigrating from Turkey to Brantford.

*Zimmerman, Leo, age 29. Farmer, emigrating from Germany to Saskatoon, Saskatchewan. Born February 20, 1883.

Author's Note

Throughout this book, I have made every effort to remain true to the facts of the *Titanic* tragedy; where information was not available, I wove in the recollections of passengers. But recreating something that happened almost 100 years ago is challenging, to say the least. The *Titanic* sank before the invention of computers, at a time when many people travelled without passports or official identification. Wealthy passengers, such as Canadian George Wright, often requested their names not be included in the ship's records. It was not unusual for emigrants, like Neshan Krekorian, for example, to sneak on board a ship without tickets. And names were sometimes recorded incorrectly (even, on occasion, spelled several different ways in the same article). For example, Thomas McCaffry's name has been variously recorded as McCaffry, McCaffery, and McCaffrey. This has obviously made it more difficult to verify the facts. So if I have made mistakes, please accept my apology. I will endeavour to correct them in future printings.

LANNY BOUTIN
(www.lannyboutin.com)

Further Reading

Adams, Simon. *Titanic.* New York: Dorling Kindersley, 1999.

Archbold, Rick and Dana McCauley. *Last Dinner on the Titanic.* New York: Madison Press, 1997.

Barczewski, Stephanie. *Titanic: A Night to Remember.* New York: Hambledon and London, 2004.

Beed, Blair. *Titanic Victims in Halifax Graveyards.* Halifax: Dtours Visitors and Convention Services, 2001.

Berton, Pierre. *The Promised Land.* Toronto: McClelland and Stewart, 1984.

Brewster, Hugh and Laurie Coulter. *882½ Amazing Answers to Your Questions About the Titanic.* Markham, Ontario: Scholastic Canada/Madison Press, 1998.

Eaton, John P. and Charles A. Haas. *Titanic: Triumph and Tragedy.* London: W. W. Norton & Company, 1994.

Esposito, Linda, senior editor. *Story of the Titanic.* New York: DK Publishing, 2001.

Garrison, Webb. *Treasury Of Titanic Tales: Stories of Life and Death from a Night to Remember.* Nashville, TN: Rutledge Hill Press, 1998.

Geller, Judith B. *Titanic: Women and Children First.* New York: W. W. Norton and Company, 1998.

Hustak, Alan. *Titanic: The Canadian Story.* Montreal: Véhicule Press, 1998.

Hyslop, Donald, Alistair Forsyth, and Sheila Jemima. *Titanic Voices.* Great Britain: Southampton City Council, 1994.

Lord, Walter. *A Night to Remember.* Mattituck, New York: Holt, Rinehart & Winston, 1987.

Lynch, Don. *Titanic: An Illustrated History.* New Jersey: Wellfleet Press, 1992.

Marriott, Leo. *Titanic.* London: PRC Publishing, 1997.

Spignesi, Stephen J. *The Complete Titanic.* Toronto: Birch Lane Press, 1998.

Molson, Karen. *The Molson's.* Willowdale, Ontario: Firefly Books, 2001.

Further Reading

Winocour, Jack, editor. *The Story of the Titanic as Told by Its Survivors: Lawrence Beesley, Archibald Gracie, Commander Lightoller, Harold Bride.* Toronto: General Publishing Company, 1960.

Acknowledgments

This book would have never happened without the great authors and researchers who went before me. I want to thank them all for helping me capture the essence of the sinking of the *Titanic*. I also want to thank the many people who helped me throughout the process. If I somehow miss mentioning you, please forgive me. Among those who gave me their invaluable assistance were: Miguel Borges (teacher, Charles Hays Secondary School, Prince Rupert, BC), Danyelle Brodeur (cultural animator, visual art, City of Dorval, Quebec), Dr. Roy Cullimore (microbiologist with Droycon Bioconcepts in Regina, Saskatchewan), Guylène Ethier (archivist, City of Dorval), Jan Melnyk for her unwavering support, Ray Huot for all his help and translations, and Barbara Schade (on behalf of the office of Mayor Sam Katz, Winnipeg, Manitoba).

My thanks also to The National Maritime Museum, Greenwich, England, holder of the Fredric A. Hamilton Diary, manuscript number JOD/221/2, for allowing parts of it to be reproduced here, (please note — I have endeavoured, without success, to track down the original copyright owner of Hamiton's diary), Dan Conlin, Curator of Marine History, Nova Scotia Museum Collections Unit, at the Maritime Museum of the Atlantic, in Halifax, Nova

Scotia, for permission to quote from "Wireless Transcript, M1998.6.1a & b," the gift of Molly Russell; the Manitoba Historical Society, and all my wonderful friends at PWAC (Professional Writers Association of Canada), who came through for me with myriad small but important facts about our great country.

I would also like to thank the wonderful contributors to *Encyclopedia Titanic*, including, but not limited to: Dennis Ahern, Andrew Aldridge, Günter Bäbler, Joan A. Barbour, Audrey Barrett, John Baxter (Quigg Baxter's nephew), George Behe, Flora Newton Brett (Ethel Fortune's first cousin), Derek Boles, the descendants of Alice Cleaver, John Clifford, Anne-Louise Coldicott, Steve Coombes, Pat Cook, Ella Deeks (Trevor Allison's cousin), Ken Deacon, Herman Dewulf, Chris Dohany, Hanna Dobrowoska, Mrs. Robert Driscoll (Mabel Fortune's daughter-in-law), Daniel Drouin, Herman DeWulf, Phillip Gowan, Tom Grassia, Linda Greaves, Michael A. Findlay, Bill Fredericks, Ruth Fox, Klaus Egvang, Pamela Hamilton, Niels L. Hoyvald, Alan Hustak, Jeffrey Kern, Peter Engberg-Klarström, Bob Knuckle, Diane Lapierre, Gerry Leacock, Pat Mayhew, Brian Meister, Olivier Mendez, Roy Mengot, Arthur Merchant, Dirk Musschoot, Hugo Normandeau, Nicholas Jardine-Pattertson, Robert Perreault, Georges Picavet, Kassandra Picavet, Michael Poirier, Suzanne Robertson, Alan Ruffman, Rob Scott, Angela Sharp, Brionee Sharp, Leif Snellman, Hermann Söldner, Alice Solomonian (Neshan Krekorian's daughter), Craig Sopin, Craig Stringer,

Brian Ticehurst, Jason D. Tiller, Alan Tucker, Len Wilkins, Geoff Whitfield, and Claes-Goran Wetterholm.

And last but not least, thanks to all the great people at Altitude Publishing who helped me realize my vision and bring this book to life, including: Joan Dixon for believing in the project, Deborah Lawson and Lesley Cameron for making it shine, and to the wonderfully talented production and design team for pulling it all together.

About the Author

Lanny Boutin is a freelance writer who specializes in health, environmental, and family-orientated stories. She writes for magazines including *Canadian Living, Treehouse Canadian Family,* and *Canadian Geographic.*

A prairie girl, born and raised in Alberta, Lanny's first book, *John Diefenbaker: The outsider who refused to quit,* was a warts-and-all chronicle of the life and times of Canada's 13th prime minister. Her second book was about mummies — the dead kind — and is called *Mummies: All Wrapped Up. Titanic: The Canadian Connection* is Lanny's third book.